Introduction to Peopleisim

Peopleisim is enacted when a majority of the people in a region simply sign the Universal Peopleisim Constitution. By far the worlds most advanced, comprehensive & eloquent Constitution, freely available to all to save Earth.

The most important characteristic of a Constitution is to optimize incentive though checks & balances, bringing maximum benefit to the people, while ensuring security on the land, with justice & prosperity for all. Peopleisim embodies the best features of democracy, socialism, capitalism & communism while avoiding the worst. Peopleisim optimizes incentives to benefit all:

- Real-time voting with a republican form of governance through Boards of Directors with an optional **democratic public override on all decisions**.
- 32 days annual Citizen Service, makes up the government including politicians, police, military, judiciary & services, **eliminating all tax**.
- **Open equal access to public & natural resources** grants top bidders lease rights, replaced at any time by a proposal with 20% higher return to the people, **eliminating corruption & maximizing the peoples income**.
- Instead of politicians deciding what to do with the people money, **income is distributed equally to each citizen**, eliminating poverty & corruption.
- Citizens **tax free Homestead** up to 2,000 m², grants security on the land.
- **Free digital education** & parents & students governing education funds.
- Innovative asynchronous adjudication & Due-Process at Common Law, Administrative Meeting, Mediation & Trial by Jury, ensures efficient **justice**.
- Intellectual property laws that **benefit** authors/inventors & open production.
- Free peoples banking & trading with asset-backed currency, **eliminates banking fraud & crimes against humanity** & invigorates the economy.
- **Restitution** & much more.

Peopleisim **ensures fairness & equity of access to public resources**, **eliminating corruption** & **maximizes the peoples income**, which **eliminates poverty**, & gives the people **security on the land**. People based governance **eliminates tax**, enabling an **economic boom,** to establish a stable sound economy, while **protecting authors & inventors** to **invigorate development** & progress. Sound asset-backed **free banking & trading eliminates fraud**, corruption & market manipulation. Innovative due-process prevents corruption in the courts, delivers **efficient & fair justice by the people for the people**.

Peopleisim delivers a new political & economic model taking advantage of the best of earlier political & economic models, wile eliminating the disadvantages. **Peopleisim is a paradigm shift** in governance, law, banking, security, intellectual property, technology, economy, education & ecology. A new Earth & new way forward, promising prosperity, peace, security & liberty for all.

Table of Contents

QUICK START
HOW TO GET PEOPLEISIM GOING IN YOUR REGION

1. Assign Guardians of the Constitution to manage the collection & safekeeping of signatures from people in your County or town.

1.1. Create your own, or download the Universal Peopleisim Constitution Signature Page from www.peopleisim.org.

1.2. Celebrate with Peopleisim Signing Parties! Collect ARTICLE 3. Ratification signatures from two thirds of the people in your area.

1.3. Optional: Report the names & number of people who sign the Universal Peopleisim Constitution to www.peopleisim.org.

2. Place former government officials on Notice to Stand Down & Declare Peopleisim as the Official Law in your County.

3. Call the people together to vote for the first County Board of Directors.

3.1. Your County Board of Directors assigns Citizen-Service including trainers to educate the people on how to take part in their new form of Peopleisim government.

3.2. Implement the functions of Peopleisim & Citizen-Services, & request Peopleisim.org to provide digital Citizen-Services in your region.

The purpose of the Copyright is to provide a common Universal Peopleisim Constitution, & cooperation between all Peopleisim regions. If you wish to change or add key elements please contact board@TheEarthPlan.com to suggest improvements, recognizing the significant effort it takes to get all regions to update to a common Constitution. **Your contributions** of time & money through www.peopleisim.org can help make this a reality. By adopting a standard Universal Peopleisim Constitution we stand together in a unified force that is impossible to hold back.

Universal Peopleisim Constitution - *Together In Unity & Love*™

UNIVERSAL PEOPLEISIM CONSTITUTION V2

All people are free & equal. In the determination of our future, we, the people, grateful for our freedom, in order to secure the blessings of justice, liberty, life, peace, security & the pursuit of happiness, & above all love, do establish this Constitution.

As opposed to Stateism where the State is declared sovereign, enslaving the people under State police, courts & military, & determining what to do with the people's money & resources; As opposed to Capitalism where Corporations are "people" who buy out politicians who rule the State which taxes the people into involuntary servitude & slavery; As opposed to Communism & Socialism where the State is declared a person, enslaving the people by taking State ownership of everything that belongs to the people. We support Peopleisim, where governance is by the people for the people; Where the earth belongs to the people; Where the peoples government distributes revenue from the peoples resources equally to each Citizen; Where Citizens own & are secure in their Homestead; Where there is no tax, no licenses, no duty; Where banking is free with a people owned asset-backed currency & bank.

We the people establish Peopleisim to take back governance to ourselves & to establish a prosperous, peaceful, sustainable & ecologically sound civilization.

ARTICLE 1. CREED

All people are by nature free & independent, & have certain inalienable rights, among which are: liberty; life; security; peace; the pursuit of happiness; justice & protection under the law; security on land, sea, space & homestead; protection from slavery, involuntary servitude & usury; protection & respect of family structure; to think & speak freely; to travel unencumbered & freely on rights-of-way; with unrestrained access to knowledge; free education; to love & be loved without interference. We the people of this Universal Peopleisim Constitution & our fellow free Citizens of all Universal Peopleisim Constitution regions enter into a firm contract of comradeship with each other, for our common defense, the security of our liberties, freedom & our mutual & general welfare, binding ourselves to assist each other, against all force or attacks made upon us on account of a pretense of democracy, stateism, fascism, socialism, capitalism, communism, religion, sovereignty, fraudulent banking systems, trade, non-representative government, or any other pretense whatsoever. We pledge our honor & service in mutual respect to bring about these goals & to love our neighbors as our selves.

ARTICLE 2. ESTABLISHMENT OF THIS UNIVERSAL PEOPLEISIM CONSTITUTION

This Universal Peopleisim Constitution shall be established by peoples signature in support here of. Firstly to the County, secondly to the Province or State, thirdly to the Nation, fourthly to the Earth, & finally to the Universe. When a majority of the adults of a County, Province, Nation or Planet have signed support hereto, this Constitution shall be declared the law of that individual & complete region.

This Constitution entirely replaces & repeals all previous Constitutions, laws, Acts of any government, codes, codex, creeds, bulls, proclamations, grants, decrees, rules, regulations & ordinances.

Citizenship lies first at the Homestead, followed by the County, Province, Nation, Planet & Universe.

ARTICLE 3. RATIFICATION

By my oath & affirmation, from Article 1 to 20, I ratify my full support of the Universal Peopleisim Constitution V2. Signature by writing, email, thumbprint or picture or online at www.peopleisim.org. Dates YYYY/M/DD:

_____Signature Date:_____

Last Name:_____

First Names:_____

Email:_____Telephone:_____

Address:_____

County/Town:_____

Province (State):_____Nation:_____

Given Name At Birth:_____Date of Birth:_____

Place of Birth:_____ Nation of Birth:_____

ARTICLE 4. DECLARATION OF RIGHTS.

Article. Section.:4.1 Supreme Law

This Constitution shall be the supreme law of the regions & higher law than Common Law.

Article. Section.:4.2 Uniform Common Law

All policies & laws shall have uniform operation. Pursuant to Common Law, the common person should be able to understand the law. Where a law is of indeterminate nature such that the common person has no way of reasonably understanding the law, the law shall be void. A limited education or poor vocabulary shall not suffice as a lack of understanding of a law, if a competent person can explain the meaning of the law.

Article. Section.:4.3 Due Process

No person shall be deprived of life, liberty, or property, without due process of law.

Article. Section.:4.4 Public Cooperation

Full Faith & Credit shall be given in each Universal Peopleisim County, Province & Nation in cooperation with all public records & proceedings. Citizens shall be equal & entitled to all Privileges & Immunities of Citizens in the many Counties. A Person properly charged in any County for a crime who flees from justice & is found in another County may be detained pursuant to the Detention Clause in this Constitution. Any lawfully mediated agreement or jury's judgment made in any County shall be respected in all Counties.

Article. Section.:4.5 Rights Shall Not Diminish

No Amendment to this constitution may eliminate rights already established in this Constitution; the rights of the people shall not diminish. No state of emergency or declaration thereof, shall eliminate or restrict the rights established in this Constitution.

Article. Section.:4.6 No Slavery Or Involuntary Servitude

Neither slavery, nor involuntary servitude shall ever be tolerated in any form.

Article. Section.:4.7 No Discrimination

Racism, including the classification of people by race or religion, shall be strictly prohibited as well as any bias against a person for their race, sex or religion.

Article. Section.:4.8 Person, People

A person is recognized as an individual soul existing on planet earth with a heartbeat. People, or persons are a collective there of. Corporations, Churches & States are not recognized as persons & retain neither authority nor sovereignty. There shall be no juristic persons nor any fictitious straw-man representation of a person. The use of upper or lower case letters to represent a person's name shall be irrelevant & simply represent the person.

Article. Section.:4.9   Protection & Respect Of Family & Individual

The right of the people to be secure without interference of their family & the absolute right of biological parents to equally enjoy & care for their children, shall not be abridged. Every child under the age of eighteen (18) has the right to nutrition, shelter, health care, education & to be protected from maltreatment, neglect, abuse or degradation, exploitative labor practices & participation in war. The right to life shall not be questioned & no person shall be subject to cruel or inhumane treatment. No person may be subjected to medical or scientific experiments without their informed & written consent.

Article. Section.:4.10   Free Knowledge & Education

All people shall have the right to freely access knowledge, to freely educate themselves & others, we the people will endeavor to bring these rights to all & make access to knowledge & learning freely available & unrestricted.

Article. Section.:4.11   Free Speech & Press

Every person may speak freely, write, express themselves & publish their sentiments on any subject, being responsible for the abuse of that right; & no policy shall be passed to restrain or abridge the liberty of expression or of any form of media. The liberty of conscience, hereby secured, shall not be so construed as to excuse indecent acts, or justify extreme practices inconsistent with the peace or safety of the people.

Where persons actively engage in the publication or broadcast of known lies & deception, or hypnosis, for the purpose of deceiving the public, their rights to utilize any public communication medium, should be limited by a competent jury or a majority of the people in a region, & they may be criminally prosecuted for racketeering & fraud. Where clear outrageous & malicious intent is obvious, & the act of deception through blatant lies is evident, & the damage caused is extensive & measurable, any Citizen may bring criminal charges against the persons behind the media, whether local or foreign.

In all criminal prosecutions on indictments for libels, the truth may be given in evidence to the mediator or jury; & if it shall appear to the mediator or jury that the matter charged as libelous is true, & was published with good motives & for justifiable ends, the accused shall be acquitted.

Article. Section.:4.12   Peaceful Gatherings & Right To Protest

The right of the people to peacefully assemble shall never be denied nor restrained, nor the right to petition for a redress of grievances.

Article. Section.:4.13   Right To Travel

The right for Citizens to travel shall be preserved as an inalienable right, & no person traveling safely without hindering others rights, shall be limited in that right by licensing, tickets, tolls, papers, road-blocks or any other means, save that expressly defined in this Constitution. Safe unhindered travel shall be measured & governed by the same Common Law standards for crime, requiring the presence of intent, the act & damage.

Citizens of established Universal Peopleisim Constitution regions shall not require passports or identity documents to travel. Where identity needs to be legitimately established, a persons County Board of Directors shall provide the necessary interface or alternatively the Citizen-Services system may be utilized pursuant to the Citizens & Identity Clause of this Constitution to verify identity. Where a traveling Citizen finds themselves in genuine difficulty, without causing any unnecessarily burden, they may approach the local County Board of Directors for assistance & as in effect, their local embassy.

For travel to Nations demanding passports, Citizens may produce their own passports of whatever design reflecting Identity necessary to travel in other non Universal Peopleisim Constitution regions.

If a visitor or traveler commits a significant crime, & is properly found guilty of the crime according to this Constitutions due process, & it is brought to the attention of the Board of Directors of that region, with good reason a majority of Directors or people may vote to expel the visitor or traveler from of their region.

Article. Section.:4.14   Ancient & Natural Wonders

Any ancient forest, tree or heritage object older than five hundred (500) years may not be destroyed or harmed. Places of significant natural beauty must be maintained in their natural state to be enjoyed by all with only reasonable limitations, to preserve their natural beauty for future generations.

Article. Section.:4.15   Religion

All people have the right to freedom of conscience, religion, thought, belief & opinion. No policy or regulation respecting an establishment of religion, or prohibiting the free exercise thereof, shall be made, except that no religion shall teach mythical stories as historical ones or promote violence & hatred. Religious claims must be backed up by sound evidence including accurate archaeological records where applicable. The same standards of hearsay applied in a court of law should also apply to religious claims.

Article. Section.:4.16   Non Fraudulent Monetary Systems

The Citizen-Services free banking, voting, trading, university & court system (Citizen-Services), shall provide an asset-backed currency, free banking & trading for the people. Except during the transition to this Constitution before the Citizen-Services Bank is available in a region, fiat-currency or fractional-reserve banking & any interest on money, shall not be permitted & may not be recognized nor utilized for any trade, loans or any purpose within the Universal Peopleisim Constitution regions. Any persons using fiat-currency or conducting fractional-reserve banking in the Universal Peopleisim Constitution regions shall be prosecuted for fraud. Notes backed by real assets of the equivalent value represented thereon, or coins of value by weight or demand, may be utilized for trade, except for lease payments on resources belonging to the people & except for any trade in natural resources. All payments for leases of the peoples resources & all trade in natural resources shall exclusively utilize the Citizen-Services currency & trading system. Any interest charged on money shall be criminally prosecuted for usury.

Article. Section.:4.17   No Titles Of Nobility, Oaths To Nefarious Organizations Or Gangs

Any Citizen who accepts, claims or retains any Title of Nobility, or shall accept & retain any Office or Emolument from any BAR Association, Emperor, King, Queen, Prince, Pope, Court, Secret Society, or undertakes an oath of allegiance to a secret or nefarious organization, shall cease to hold Citizenship or any of the benefits there of & shall be incapable of holding any Office public or private. Those who serve in public office while under a blood oath to a nefarious or secret organization, shall be prosecuted for treason. No nefarious gangs, societies, orders or associations shall be allowed that established orders or hierarchies of control that give preference to their members in a court of law, or in regard to any public matter, including general business. On signing this Constitution, each & every Citizen waives, gives up & annuls any oath, vow, pledge or enslavement to any secret or nefarious organization or gang. Citizens as a whole pledge to harbor & protect each & every Citizen from secret or nefarious organizations & gangs.

Article. Section.:4.18   No War

We the people will not partake in, aid, fund or promote any invasion, torture or genocide, nor assist in any such endeavor. We will not declare war, other than in defense to an act of war directly against us. Any declaration of war in defense of an act of war, must be approved by at least a two thirds majority of the Citizens from a region, in a vote called specifically for that purpose, recognizing that often the best form of defense, is to dodge an attack or be able to take the blow, & recognizing that shooting with a camera verses a gun, allows the shot to be replicated world wide repeatedly for all too witness. Invasions under the guise of defensive action shall not be tolerated. At no time shall any person, association, militia or military utilize weapons for a show of force to threaten or oppress persons who are no serious & nefarious danger to the people. The promotion of violence through media shall be prohibited. No standing army shall be kept or funded in times of peace; & in time of defense, no army shall be formed or funded for a period longer than two years. The militia & military shall in all instances be subordinate to the people & may not act without the direct approval of two thirds of the people. The people shall not be prohibited from securing their personal security, however security shall not be used to establish private armies, which shall be prohibited.

Article. Section.:4.19   Right To Own & Carry Guns/Arms

The right to defend oneself from crime & oppression is an inalienable right. The right of Citizens to own, keep & carry weapons for defense, shall not be infringed. Non-Citizens may not own, carry, use or have access to any weapon, including any remotely controlled weapon, in any Universal Peopleisim Constitution region.

Citizens may own weapons for defense, however, if more than half a County or one quarter of a Province vote to disarm any individual, that person shall respect their neighbors & immediately get rid of their weapons, or never enter the region that voted to disarm them.

Article. Section.:4.20   No Search Or Seizure Without Probable Cause & Oath Or Affirmation

The privacy of an individuals person, home, property, possessions, & communications shall be respected & not infringed. The right of the people to be secure in their persons, houses, papers, communication & effects, against unreasonable searches & seizures, shall not be violated. No Warrants shall be issued other than Warrants signed by at least six qualified jurors, where significant evidence indicates genuine probable cause of a serious & significant crime, supported by an Oath or Affirmation by a real party of interest, & describing in detail the place to be searched, methods & times allowed, & the persons or things to be seized. Those requesting, approving & conducting a search or seizure, shall be liable for damages if they unfairly violate a persons rights secured by this Constitution.

Article. Section.:4.21   Detention

No person shall be delayed or detained without proper cause. No person shall be unreasonably delayed from their business, travel or pleasure for more than five minutes. No person shall be detained for more than 24 hours without a Grand Jury Indictment. Neither an accused, witness or evidence shall be unreasonably detained. No person or property shall be unreasonably detained or seized without just compensation.

Where a lawful Indictment & warrant for arrest exists for a person & that person is accurately identified, any Citizen may detain the accused for up to twenty four hours (24h), pursuant to the terms of the arrest warrant, for those issuing the warrant to collect the accused. However, the person/s detaining the accused holds a duty to the accused to ensure the warrant is properly issued with good cause & only for a serious crime. If the warrant is for an order to appear before a jury, the accused must be given the option to sign an agreement to appear on a specific date before the jury, which if they sign or give a videotaped agreement to appear, they must be immediately released.

Article. Section.:4.22   Real Parties

Only real parties of interest may bring charges before a Jury. A real party of interest is any victim who suffered damage in the accused crime, or in a civil case a person with a direct ownership or interest in the matter. A guardian may also be considered a real party of interest, if a real party of interest is not able to file charges. In no instances is the State a real party of interest.

Article. Section.:4.23   Grand Jury & Warrants

No person may be arrested or held to answer for a crime, unless on presentment or indictment of a people's Grand Jury made up of twenty four (24) individuals from the region where the crime was allegedly committed & where a majority of the Jury find clear & obvious probable cause for the charges. An arrest to restrain a person before a trial must only be allowed in extreme cases where the crime is exceptionally serious & the flight risk is very high & in cases where failing to restrain the person, is highly likely to result in the suspect committing murder or causing very serious damage. Serious damage in this instance shall amount to the loss of life, limb or property damage in excess of what the accused is able to pay in restitution & at least in excess of ten kilograms of gold (10 kgG).

The accused shall, if they choose, have the opportunity to appear before, question & appeal to the Grand Jury to reverse their indictment or presentment. Grand Juror's hold a duty to act diligently, with integrity & justly & in conformance with the law, & are personally liable for unreasonable actions.

Article. Section.:4.24 Administrative Meeting

Mediation & trials shall be preceded by an Administrative Meeting, with the opportunity given to all parties to attended, who shall attempt to resolve the dispute without the burden of Mediation or a Trial by Jury.

Article. Section.:4.25 Only Jury Power In All Trials

Judicial power shall never exist in any form or court. Decisions shall be made with consent in Mediation, or by the jury in a Trial By Jury.

Article. Section.:4.26 Jury Determines Law & Fact

Based on this Constitution & Common Law, the jury shall judge both the law & the fact in all cases.

Article. Section.:4.27 No Lawful Trial Shall Be Retried

No fact properly tried by a jury, shall be re-examined in any Court other than according to the rules of this Constitution & Common Law. No person shall be tried more than once for the same offense, save where it can be clearly proven that the accused blatantly & intentionally violated the due process clauses of this Constitution for the purpose of changing the outcome of the trial.

Article. Section.:4.28 Writ Of Habeas Corpus

The privilege of the writ of Habeas Corpus shall never be suspended & shall be honored by Grand Juries, Juries & the Boards of Directors.

Article. Section.:4.29 Reasonable Bail

The Grand Jury issuing the arrest warrant shall be responsible for setting bail requirements & also liable to an extent for releasing an arrested person who is a serious & obvious risk. Excessive bail shall be prohibited. All arrested persons shall be bailable, by sufficient & reasonable sureties; unless for capital offenses, when the proof is clearly evident or the presumption great & the accused remains a serious threat to other individuals lives. The accused must be permitted to provide any real asset as surety. Where a financial bail deposit is utilized, the funds shall be held in the Peopleisim General-Fund, & with proper certification, issued without delay from the Peopleisim General-Fund when released.

Article. Section.:4.30   Overwhelming Evidence In Criminal Trials

In criminal trials a person shall only be found guilty of criminal charges if all twelve of twelve jurors are completely convinced that there is overwhelming evidence proving the accused is guilty.

Article. Section.:4.31   No Courts Of Equity or Admiralty Courts

There shall be no courts of equity or admiralty courts whatsoever. Where a remedy at law does not exist as a consequence of one party to a case being unable to take part in the legal process, a qualified guardian shall be appointed by the closest relative, if no relative exists the closest best friend, if no best friend exists the Board of Directors shall appoint a qualified guardian in the interests of the person or entity who has no possibility of representing themselves, & said case shall conform to the Due Process prescribed herein.

Article. Section.:4.32   Non Oppressive Courts

No fancy or strange dress code, such as black cloaks or wigs, shall be allowed in the Courts. The Court layout shall strictly not give anyone a psychological disadvantage or advantage. Absolutely no high-fluting or ridiculous titles shall be used in addressing any person in a Court.

Article. Section.:4.33   Speedy Fair Criminal Trial

In all criminal prosecutions, the accused shall enjoy the right to a speedy, fair & public trial preceded by an Administrative Meeting & Mediation pursuant to the Due Process of this Constitution.

Article. Section.:4.34   Fully Informed; Right To Witnesses & Counsel

In all cases, the accused shall be fully informed of the nature & cause of the accusation/s filed against them; have access to all the information in the case; be able to question the witnesses; have compulsory process for obtaining witnesses & evidence in their favor, & to have unlimited assistance of their counsel/s for their defense if they so choose. If a defendant can not afford counsel for their defense, as part of their Citizens Service a competent counselor shall be appointed to assist the defendant by the Citizen-Services Universal Common Law Court or the local County Board of Directors. If the defendant can prove that the appointed counsel is not competent, the defendant may appeal to the jury or the Provincial Board of Directors either of which shall examine the evidence & appoint an alternate qualified counsel if necessary.

Article. Section.:4.35   Compulsory Evidence

Those prosecuting a case & witnesses shall not hold any evidence from the accused that in any way relates to the charges & said evidence shall be given to the accused as soon as possible.

Article. Section.:4.36   Right To Record, Speak & Present Evidence

Save any specific lawful demand by the parties, mediators or jury, for a synchronous hearing with the parties present, the parties shall be allowed to appear with or without counsel via electronic means conforming to Citizen-Services standard digital formats for documents, pictures, audio & video. In any situation, the right to record, speak & present evidence using any & multiple unobtrusive means of recording & presenting the evidence shall never be denied. There shall be no limitation placed on the party's choice of counsel/s or any rights of their counsel/s to present the case. The jury holds the right to judge the case & issue final judgment in their own time. Consequentially, parties to a case naturally should not waste the jury's time.

In a court of law, there is no right to remain silent, nor any right to hide the truth through any client secrecy or confidentiality privileges. A counselor may be called to testify as a witness in a case. Justice in law makes no leeway for secrecy or hiding the truth for the purpose of distorting justice. However if a person does not know an answer, they cannot be compelled to make one up. The jury is free to interpret the failure to answer a question in light of all the facts surrounding a case.

Article. Section.:4.37   Jury Duty

All Citizens & Residents over the age of eighteen (18) agree to act as jurors in trials brought under this Constitution. If jury duty exceeds the thirty two (32) days Citizen Service in a year, reasonable restitution may be arranged by the local County Board of Directors to be paid voluntarily for by the local community. Jury duty may be counted as annual Citizen-Service. Over & above their annual thirty two days service, professional Jurors may also volunteer or offer their services for a fee.

Jurors shall be able to examine the evidence & arguments to a case online in their own time, except on occasions when parties to a case demand a synchronous hearing & six (6) or more jurors agree to a synchronous hearing where all shall be present at a location, date & time mutually reasonable to all involved in the case. When any party to a case is unreasonable in setting up or attending a synchronous hearing, six or more jurors may dictate a time, date & place for the hearings.

Once jurors have examined the evidence & have made a sound decision, they individually submit their ruling & reasoning for said ruling to the Common Law Court on the Citizen-Services system which will coordinate & expedite the conclusion of said rulings where necessary and/or request jurors to reexamine evidence where necessary. Once a majority of jurors in a civil case, & all jurors in a criminal case, are in agreement, a singular joint judgment shall be issued by the jury. A majority of jurors in a civil case & all jurors in a criminal case may conclude the case when any of the parties to the case is exceptionally unreasonable in answering or prosecuting the case. The jury & parties to a case shall make every effort to complete the case in a reasonable time. If a jury is unable to make a decision within six months of all parties to a case concluding their argument, any party to the case my request a new jury.

Article. Section.:4.38   Liability In Trials

All parties to a trial, including the real party of interest, jurors, accused & witnesses, are liable for their respective actions or failure to act reasonably; the parties in speaking & producing the truth; the jury in judging fairly & impartially.

Article. Section.:4.39   No Excessive Fine Or Cruel Punishment

Excessive fines or penalties shall not be imposed, nor shall cruel & unusual punishment be inflicted.

Without consequence, there is no accountability, without accountability there is no justice. The general community, & not the victim, should take on the responsibility of enforcing consequence, to ensure the peoples conscience remains aware & pure. Punishment should be metered with love in mind, taking into account the release of the victim & the reformation of the criminal. Our every act makes up the essence of our soul, what we do, cannot be undone.

Article. Section.:4.40   Captivity Only For Capital Offenses

No person shall be held captive as punishment, unless that person is found guilty in a lawful Trail By Jury of a Capital Offense, & the guilty party is likely to commit another Capital Offense if released. Detention prior to & during trial shall only be permitted for extreme capital offenses where the evidence of guilt is overwhelming & the danger of release extreme & obvious. Punishment shall be in the form of restitution to the victims & their families and/or fines to be paid into the Peopleisim General-Fund and/or in public service to correct the offenders bad behavior, except, where necessary, the guilty may also be limited to a specified Badlands region for a reasonable length of time determined by the jury.

Article. Section.:4.41   Punishment For Crime & Restitution

No person shall be punished without due process of law as defined in this Constitution. The practice of placing criminals in a jail or prison shall be avoided as this tends to incite the criminal element. More effective punishment must be enforced by juries so as to ensure the reformation of the criminal to a good contributing member of society & in restitution directly to victims of the crime. Where the crime is serious & the risk to others if the criminal is released is severe, & strict reformation of the criminal is necessary, the Badlands Clause of this Constitution should be utilized for confinement.

The death penalty should be avoided at all costs, & only ruled where proof of an extremely heinous crime is absolute without any shadow of doubt whatsoever, & where there is absolutely no chance the person will ever reform; & only instituted after every affordable appeal is exhausted. If it is ever determined conclusively that a jury was negligent in their duty & they issued the death penalty, the jurors themselves shall be subject to trial & the death penalty. Any person who threatens or injures a juror or mediator in relation for their judgment on a case, may be subject to the most severe penalty up to & including the death penalty.

Article. Section.:4.42 Political Parties

While general cooperation amongst Citizens & Directors shall not be prohibited, Political Parties shall be prohibited. Any person standing for office shall stand on their own merits.

Article. Section.:4.43 Labor Unions & Management

No law shall prohibit or enforce the voluntary organization or management of labor.

Article. Section.:4.44 Integrity & Safety In Employment

Employers shall respect employees rights to reasonable compensation & at least a living wage along with a safe work environment. Where known hazards exist, employers must take the necessary precautions to ensure the safety of employees & all.

Article. Section.:4.45 Integrity

It is the right of every person to expect other people to act with integrity. Where a lawfully formed jury finds an accused guilty of a significant lack of integrity for an outrageous offense, & there is clear & obvious intent to defraud or steal or maliciously harm the victim, respecting no Cruel Punishment, the jury should treat the guilty person with a proverbial iron fist that ensures the guilty party & others will act with honesty, respect & integrity. Further offense is added when a person in the wrong does not reasonably settle in mediation & allows the matter to be taken to trial by jury.

Article. Section.:4.46 Integrity In Medicine

Medical professionals are bound to a duty of care to their patients, to not administer any medicine or treatment that is likely to harm the patient; To not refuse medical aid in an emergency; To not overcharge patients for any treatment; To not refuse medical treatment to any patient for any racial, religious or sexist reason; To not engage in any life threatening activity against people or the planet; To not participate in any body-part trade other than what is freely donated with the written & informed consent of the donor; To maintain a persons medical records & issues in confidence, save that which proposes a serious risk of plague to the greater populous, which shall be disclosed in confidence to the Boards of Directors of the affected region who shall have a duty to act sensibly in the interests of the people. Following full Due Process conforming to criminal law standards, where the entire immediate family & grandchildren participate & are present, & the person's Will & Last Testament is carefully considered, with a Trial By Jury's verdict & authority, euthanasia may be granted & professionally administered.

Article. Section.:4.47   Integrity In Agriculture & Food

The use of any pesticides, hormones, hazardous chemicals & substances, or potentially harmful genetically modified foods, must be fully disclosed along with any health risks to the consumer. The production of crops & produce that are known to cause significant health risks, may be criminally prosecuted by any affected person/s. The farmer, producer, middlemen & sellers of any food are responsible & liable for damages the consumption of their food causes where those damages could have & should have been reasonably understood & properly forewarned and/or prevented.

Article. Section.:4.48   Integrity In Genetic Engineering

Mankind having reached a level of knowledge where scientists can create new plants and animals species, a function primitive man attributed to "god", must recognize & acknowledge the awesome responsibility such knowledge carries. What if some unethical scientist engineered a species that killed & ate every other species on the planet? Or what if the elite engineered tasty crops that slowly sterilized and killed anyone they wanted to get rid of? What if some dictator got his scientists to engineer a biological weapon that wiped out anyone without his antidote? These are all now possible.

Genetic engineering shall be prohibited which harms beings. Any and all genetic engineering will exclusively focus on the care of life & the protection of all beings in love. Any person found funding, supporting or engaging in genetic engineering that significantly harms people, shall be prosecuted and sent to the Badlands for a length of time necessary to eliminate their threat.

Article. Section.:4.49   Mind Altering Substances

The producer, middlemen & sellers of any narcotic or mind controlling substance is responsible & liable for the proper use of the substance including any consequential damages uncontrolled users may cause. A warning on the package will not suffice. The sale of mind altering substances to minors without their parent or guardians written & informed permission, is prohibited & may be criminally prosecuted by the parents or guardians of the minors & or the general community.

Article. Section.:4.50   Labeling

Producers & sellers of products that have known or potential dangerous effects or side effects, must to the best of their ability reasonably & clearly disclose the nature of the ingredients of the product & the known & potential dangers of the product in the sales process & labeling of the product, to ensure the consumer is properly educated & aware of any potential or known dangerous effects.

Article. Section.:4.51   Internet

No law or system shall bar access to Internet, Internet Domains or communication over public networks. No law or system shall dictate how private networks & systems are set up & managed. Anyone, including individuals,

Associations & Universities may setup private networks. Internet search engines shall not censor content without explicitly publishing the details of their censorship algorithms, keywords & black lists.

Article. Section.:4.52   Trademarks

Genuinely unique trademarks shall be recognized & respected for their specific category of industry for the significant life & regions the product is directly sold to, protected according to the first publication of the Trademark's use by placing "TM" next to said Trademark as such: TrademarkName™.

Article. Section.:4.53   Copyrights & Patents

The purpose of any copyright or patent is to promote the media, idea or design by directly rewarding the author/inventor. Copyrights or patents fail when they are used as a form of blackmail to reward people other than the author or inventor. Patent systems have largely been utilized to censor & limit advanced technology by large conglomerates & corrupt governments, to shut out competitors & to enslave the masses with outdated technology & by placing Gag-Orders on advanced new technology, including but not limited to anti-gravity & free energy systems. To lock up an idea is to lock up progress. However, for example, the person who teaches a criminal how to build an atomic bomb, partakes in the crime when there is damage as a consequence; in some instances people can be liable for what they publish or teach. The former Patent System shall be abolished & not recognized nor respected. Copyrighting of text, audio, video (collectively referred to as "media"), ideas & designs shall be recognized for the purpose of rewarding authors & inventors when their media, idea or design is reproduced for sale.

- A copyright of a complete original media shall last twenty five (25) years.
- A copyright of a complete original design shall last ten (10) years.
- A copyright of a complete original idea shall last seven (7) years.

To copyright a product the copyright mark © followed by the original date of creation & the person or organization who created & owns the copyright must be placed on the product as such: "© 2014 CopyrightOwner", in addition to any specific restrictions, limitations or permissions & the annual royalty for single or multiple reproductions, or a website address where the precise reproduction terms can be found if the Copyright Owner name is not a website itself. The terms of reproduction should not be vague. Any person or Association may utilize a copyright for reproduction by paying the copyright royalties to the copyright owner. At least fifty percent (50%) of the royalties for any copyright must go directly to the person/s who authored or invented the work. Copyright rights may be published for sale on the Citizen-Services Trading System. Where less than twenty percent (20%) of a copyrighted product is replicated in a product, no royalty shall be due. Data lawfully accessed off a public Internet & stored in a devices cache for improved network performance shall not be considered a violation of a copyright. The protection of a copyright shall follow standard civil Due-Process:

- Where it can be show that the media existed twenty five (25) years beforehand in any field, the copyright or non-original portion thereof shall be void.

- Where it can be show that the design existed ten (10) years beforehand in any field, the copyright or non-original portion thereof shall be void.

- Where it can be show that the idea existed five (5) years beforehand in any field, the copyright or non-original portion thereof shall be void.

By replicating a copyrighted product a person accepts liability & a duty to pay the royalties on the product at the time of replication. Failure to pay may incur penalties due to the author or inventor & in serious violations, fines payable to the Peopleisim General-Fund as determined through standard Due-Process.

Article. Section.:4.54 Acknowledgment, Signatures & Verification

Acknowledgment of an agreement may be accomplished by various types of signatures to the necessary level of verification as specified or required by the magnitude of the contract. Written, digital or biological signatures may be captured & verified through various means, including handwritten signature, email address, IP address, telephone number, face, body, finger print/s, retina, handwriting, picture, voice, video, DNA or by use of a unique identity device including an identity document, card or chip & the establishment of location through GPS, routing or picture, with various time stamps.

ARTICLE 5. DUE PROCESS, UNIVERSAL COMMON LAW COURT: ADMINISTRATIVE MEETING, MEDIATION & TRIAL BY JURY

This Constitution enacts the implementation of distributed Universal Common Law Courts managed by the people to facilitate Administrative Hearings, Mediation & Common Law Trial by Jury, with the opportunity for Asynchronous & Synchronous filing, hearings & adjudication. BAR Association Court systems, Admiralty Courts, & Courts of Equity are prohibited. All agreements, contracts & commerce shall conform to this Constitution & Common Law.

Definition of Synchronous & Asynchronous Meetings & Hearings

Synchronous meetings are conducted with all parties present either physically at one place or present virtually at the same time, typically conducted over a relatively short period of minuets or hours.

Asynchronous meetings are conducted without out the parties present, where participants can be distributed over many locations & are able to communicate asynchronously at different times over the course of the meeting (with for example email or on a website blog), over a period of hours, days, weeks, or longer.

Article. Section.:5.1 Administrative Meeting

Any & all legal action will be preceded with a formal Common Law Administrative Meeting between all parties; The person bringing the matter forward shall schedule & invite the other parties to the Administrative Meeting which shall be scheduled to take place at a reasonable location & time suitable to all parties. The purpose of the Administrative meeting is to get the parties to communicate their grievances in an attempt to mutually resolve the case. If the matter is not settled in the Administrative Meeting, the parties shall enter into formal non-binding Mediation. Following the Mediators recommendations a second Administrative Meeting shall be scheduled by the Mediator/s in an attempt to obtain an agreed resolution, if the matter can still not be settled, the matter may be moved to a formal Trial By Jury.

Article. Section.:5.2 Non-binding Mediation

In civil cases, both parties may stipulate to binding mediation. Criminal cases require a Grand Jury Indictment to proceed with this stage. The person prosecuting the case shall be called the "Applicant", the person defending the case shall be called the "Respondent".

Under an oath that their concerted efforts to solve the issue in an Administrative Meeting failed, an Applicant may open a case on the Citizen-Services Court System against a Respondent. The Applicant/s, Respondent/s & their Counselor/s shall be issued unique Citizen-Services Court System email addresses to be used exclusively for the case. If the Respondent does not voluntarily respond, the Applicant must ensure that a Citizen-Services Court Summons is served directly to the Respondent/s in person by an independent & competent individual who shall submit a proof of service under oath on the Citizen-Service Court system. If the respondent claims that no Administrative Meeting has taken place, the Respondent must set a date for one within ten (10) days of acknowledging the case or receiving the summons, after which the case shall commence mediation if it is not resolved.

The parties shall mutually select a qualified mediator on the Citizen-Services Court System, if they cannot agree on the same mediator, they shall each select their own mediator within ten (10) days of the Respondent acknowledging the case or being served the Summons.

If thirty (30) days after the Respondent acknowledged the case or was properly served a Citizen-Services Summons for the case, & at least thirty (30) days after the Applicant has properly & comprehensively completed filing evidence & arguments, the Respondent refuses to participate in mediation, the Mediator both parties selected or the Applicant's Mediator if the Respondent did not select one, may call a Mediators Administrative Meeting stating mediation has failed & allow the Applicant to proceed to Trial by Jury.

The parties shall proceed to make their case by filing evidence, argument & answers into the Citizen-Services Court System for the mediator/s to evaluate.

There shall be no limitations on submission of relevant evidence to a case, which shall be broadly accepted, including reference to on-line information as long as the information is easily accessible by all parties, mediator/s & jurors for the full duration of mediation, trial & any subsequent appeal, save Citizen-Services specifying standard file formats & stipulating that all material filed be free of viruses, Trojans or any malicious software. Where physical evidence is submitted, at the expense of the submitting party, the mediator shall store the evidence in a Citizen-Services approved secure location suitable for the type of evidence, & make the evidence reasonably available for inspection by either party, experts, or the Jury if the case goes to Trial By Jury. The party submitting physical evidence may hold the evidence so long as they reasonably present it for the other party, mediator, juror or expert to examine on request.

The mediator/s may interview & call the parties to meetings which shall be suitably recorded. The mediator & parties to the case are responsible for expediting the case. Mediators must allow parties at least ten (10) days to file answers & mediators may allow more time when a party provides convincing evidence that they cannot reasonably meet a deadline. All parties to a case may rate & comment on the mediators service.

Once the mediator/s is/are satisfied that the case has been properly presented, answered & filed, they shall call a Mediators Administrative Meeting to propose a settlement. If the Mediators Administrative Meeting fails to resolve the case, it may be brought to Trial By Jury. For a Trial By Jury to proceed, proper evidence & argument must have been filed in the mediation phase.

Article. Section.:5.3 Common Law Trial By Jury

Following a failed Mediators Administrative Meeting, the Applicant may bring the case to a Trial By Jury if it has been properly filed during mediation. Where parties to a case have been negligent in filing evidence & argument during mediation, by a majority vote Juries may choose to restrain parties from filing new evidence or argument during the Trail by Jury. By a majority vote of a Jury, the case may also be sent back to mediation if it has not been properly filed during mediation.

In Civil cases the parties may agree on the size of the Jury between three (3) & twelve (12) jurors, if they cannot agree, the number shall be set at six (6). Criminal trials shall have twelve (12) jurors. Civil trials that incorporate criminal elements may be conducted simultaneously with twelve (12) jurors pursuant to the civil & criminal jury requirements. A sequence of potential jurors shall be randomly selected by the Citizen-Services Court System from Citizens preferably from the region where the crime or dispute occurred; to test if jurors qualify, parties to a case may ask potential jurors any relevant question via email which the potential jurors must answer within two (2) working days; With all parties present, recorded video conferencing may also be utilized to question potential jurors; All jurors must qualify for impartiality & competence. Allowing for expert testimony, jurors must qualify to judge the facts & law relating to the charges, including the act, damage & Intent; Where intent is a significant issue & questionable, the Jury shall be made up of jurors who are qualified to understand the mind of the accused; Where parties to a case challenge the qualifications of a potential juror, after a minimum of four jurors have been approved by both parties, a vote of three quarters of the seated Jury may dismiss a challenge they consider unreasonable; If a party challenges the qualification of one hundred potential jurors before four jurors have been seated, they must select four jurors from those that the other party has approved. The parties to a case may dismiss up to four qualified jurors for no reason; Once the required number plus two reserve jurors have been selected by the proceeding method & if the jurors are local, the parties may request a synchronous hearing to finalize Jury selection.

The Trial By Jury shall be conducted dynamically both asynchronously & synchronously, employing asynchronous electronic means where possible. Where parties reasonably demand & require synchronous hearings physically before the Jury, with the approval of at least three jurors, it must be granted. Three or more jurors may also demand synchronous hearings where all jurors are present for discussion. Three or more jurors may demand synchronous hearings to examine the parties & witnesses at which all parties shall be present. The Jury Foreman shall arrange suitable times, dates an locations for synchronous hearings.

Once seated, each juror shall be issued a unique Citizen-Services Court System email address to use exclusively for the case & the Jury shall by a majority vote elect a Jury Foreman from amongst them, who along with the Jury, shall ensure the case moves forward properly & efficiently. By a majority vote of the jurors a new Jury Foreman may be appointed at any point through the trial. Each juror shall immediately start independently evaluating the evidence & argument filed by the parties on the Citizen-Services Court System, communicating their findings & questions amongst the other jurors exclusively utilizing their case specific Citizen-Services Court System email address. Jurors may request information from the parties & may conduct their own investigations into the matters which they shall share with other jurors & all parties to the case. Jurors may ask the parties of a case any relevant question via email or in person during a synchronous hearing, which must be recorded & answered. With reasonable limitations, jurors may also file relevant evidence & argument in a case.

To expedite a case, the Jury Foreman may demand either party or jurors respond to specific request within ten (10) days. Once jurors reach a verdict they submit it into the Citizen-Services Court System. The Jury Foreman may instruct jurors to conduct further investigation or reconsider their verdict or decision. The Jury Foreman shall be responsible for finding & publishing the median verdict & decision from the jurors. In a Civil case when a majority & in a criminal case when all the jurors vote to approve the common verdict & decision published by the Jury Foreman, the trials verdict & decision shall be finalized. All parties to a case may publicly rate & comment on jurors service.

Based on the Jury's ruling, the losing party may be require to pay reasonable costs for the trial in addition to restitution and/or fines. Those found not guilty in criminal trials should be entitled to reasonable costs for defense & damages governed by the Jury's ruling & payable by the parties that brought the case against them. Those subject to Malicious Prosecution should be entitled to double their reasonable defense costs & double any damages suffered as a consequence of the malicious prosecution, payable by the parties maliciously prosecuting the case & determined by the Jury. The Jury may fine any person bringing a frivolous case to trial. Any fines imposed by a Jury shall be paid into the Peopleisim General-Fund.

In criminal trials where the accused is found guilty of a heinous crime such as murder & is still a threat to other individuals or to society in general, the Jury should determine a course of action to restrain & reform the guilty party until they are no longer a threat. The concept of jails & prisons is highly discouraged & shall be replaced by the Badlands clause of this Constitution.

Article. Section.:5.4 Appeals & Appellate Jury

The people shall have the right to appeal to an Appellate Jury to determine whether any criminal trial, or a civil trial where a Jury made an awarded valued at more than the equivalent of ten grams (10gg) of gold, conformed to the Due Process dictated in this Constitution & Common Law. Appellate Juries shall consist of twelve (12) competent individuals of high moral character & unquestionable integrity who have no personal interest in any of the parties of a trial in question. Appellate Jurors must be capable & qualified to judge the conformance of a trial to the Due Process dictated by this Constitution. As with all jurors, Appellate jurors are required to act with compete integrity, fairly & impartially & are also liable for any negligence or misconduct.

Appellate Juries shall be formed in the same manner as Trial By Juries. Any Appellate Jury's decisions to set aside a Trial by Jury's decision, must be unanimous & based on proof beyond a reasonable doubt. If a trial at question is found by the Appellate Jury to significantly violate the Due Process Laws of this Constitution & Common Law that would have resulted in a reversed or potentially reversed outcome, & thus the party making the appeal was denied a fair trial, the Appellate Jury shall annul the decision of the original Trial By Jury & if necessary order another trial, except that no person denied a fair criminal trial shall be subject to another trial for the same offense. Appellate Juries shall have the power within their discretion to answer & approve writs of Habeas Corpus for any person held captive. Appellate Juries may impose fines payable to the Peopleisim General-Fund on any person making a frivolous appeal.

Article. Section.:5.5 Voter Appeal

If more than fifty percent of a County's Voters vote against the outcome of a trial, with the approval of a majority of the Provincial & National Board of Directors, the outcome of that trial shall be annulled.

ARTICLE 6. MAXIMS AT COMMON LAW:

The following Maxims at Common Law shall be respected by all:

- A maxim is so called because its dignity is highest, its authority most certain, & because it is universally approved.

- Society does not need rule & code books, they need good measures to live by. "To love" is a good measure, "to hate" is bad, "to do harm" is bad, "to care" is good. Weigh up actions. Be good.

Government

- If you don't govern yourself someone else will.
- If a people will not govern themselves they guarantee their own enslavement.
- The government is to be subject to the law, for the law makes government.
- If the people do not know how to form, manage & control their own juries & courts, politicians & lawyers will rise up to corrupt justice.
- Public servants purpose is to serve.
- To any person who exceeds their office or jurisdiction, no obedience is due.
- Tyranny & oppression only survive where there is apathy, fear & indifference.
- Those who let the waters of corruption pass under their bridge, flood their neighbors.
- Power is not conferred, but for the public good.

Justice & Innocence

- Do not judge if you do not understand.
- No man should be condemned unheard.
- Justice is neither to be denied nor delayed.
- Hasty justice risks injustice.
- Everyone is presumed to be innocent until their guilt is established beyond a reasonable doubt.
- All things are presumed to be lawfully done & duly performed until the contrary is proved.
- There can be no crime unless there is an intentional criminal act that causes real damage.
- Every act is to be estimated by the intention of the doer.
- An act that causes damage does not make a person a criminal, unless their intent is also criminal.
- Punishment must never precede a crime.
- No one can be convicted for thoughts.
- An arrest without a Grand Jury Indictment, implements tyranny.

- Significant probable cause must proceed a Grand Jury indictment or presentment.
- The burden of proof lies upon him who makes the charge, not on him who denies the charge.
- When the plaintiff does not prove their case, the defendant is absolved.
- The foundation of justice is a fair trial. If any of the following fails the affirmative, the trial is not fair & void on its face:
    1. An impartial qualified jury;
    2. No exclusion of relevant evidence or testimony;
    3. Competent parties or counsel.
- With sound mind & logic reasoning, setting aside emotion, a competent jury enacts justice.
- No person shall be judge in their own cause, especially the State.
- Corruption & injustice parallel the amount of benefit a judge receives from their ruling.
- To judge without knowing the relevant facts is called ignorance, in a court of law it is called malpractice.
- In a criminal case a unanimous jury must find proof of guilt beyond any reasonable doubt.
- No person ought to be burdened in consequence of another persons act.
- In things to favor, what does good is more regarded than what does harm.
- One making a voluntary confession, is to be dealt with more mercifully.
- It is better the guilty go free than the innocent be punished.
- It is safer to err on the side of mercy.
- Incentive ensures justice or injustice.

Defense, Evidence & Witnesses

- The function of a legal counselor is not for the purpose of distorting justice, it is to ensure justice.
- The faculty & right of offering proof, is not to be narrowed.
- No one is restrained from using several defenses.
- In law, none is credited unless they are sworn. All the facts must, when established by witnesses, be under oath or affirmation.
- A person's innocence or guilt is determined by evidence. Deny the evidence, & the innocent are convicted & guilty go free.
- Only real parties of interest can bring an action to court.
- A mere appearance does not imply consent.
- Truth delivers justice.

- A liar is a thief of truth.
- To lie is to go against the mind.
- Truth fears nothing but concealment.
- Suppression of the truth is equivalent to the expression of what is false.
- Suppression of fact, which should be disclosed, is the same in effect as willful misrepresentation.
- It is difficult to make written evidence lie & harder to make video taped evidence lie.
- Two eye witnesses are better than ten ear ones.
- Hearsay is questionable evidence.
- Facts are more powerful than words.
- Words are to be interpreted according to the subject-matter.
- He who considers merely the letter of an instrument, goes but skin deep into its meaning.
- When the words & the mind agree, there is no place for interpretation.
- Examples illustrate, they do not restrict the law.
- Definite legal conclusions, cannot be made on hypothetical theories.
- That which was originally void, does not by lapse of time become valid.
- Time a crime does not erode. Statutes of limitation are anti-law.

Accountability

- Without accountability there can be no justice. Consequence ensures accountability.
- The deterrent of punishment starves off the incentive to commit a crime.
- Multiplied by intent, the consequence of a crime should amount to or exceed the act & damage.
- Those that incur the benefit incur the cost.
- An accident does not carry intent.
- Inaction can be as criminal as action.
- The one who turns a blind eye on crime participates in it.
- The silence of the good is more deafening than the shouts of evil.
- It is better to suffer every wrong or ill, than to consent to it.
- It is better to recede than to proceed wrongly.
- Remove the cause & the effect will cease.
- It is not lawful to do evil that good may come of it.
- He who commands a thing to be done, is held to have done it himself.
- The multitude of those who do wrong, is no excuse for doing wrong.
- No one ought to enrich themselves, at the expense of others.

- If a beneficiary imposes taxes or fines, what prevents corruption?
- Do those who claim to speak on behalf of an invisible mute god, speak for themselves?
- Honor & Integrity know no hierarchy.

Ownership & Contracts

- The agreement makes the contract.
- The contract makes the law.
- Every consent involves a submission; but a mere submission does not necessarily involve consent.
- A contract founded on a base & unlawful consideration, or against good morals, is null.
- Let the buyer & seller beware.
- One cannot transfer to another a right they do not have.
- A person who has possession & right to property, holds a double right, forming a complete title.
- What is mine cannot be taken away without my consent.
- Possessions taken or captured by pirates, robbers, fraud or by war, does not change ownership, & the possessions do not become the lawful property of the captors.
- The length of time possessed does not negate theft nor the rights of the owner.
- Every person's Homestead is their castle & security.
- The habitation of each one is their inviolable asylum.
- Enjoy your own property in such a manner so as not to injure another persons property.
- The law which governs corporations is the same as that which governs individuals.
- A corporation cannot be used to veil individual responsibility to avoid accountability.

Life & Law

- Law is the dictate of reason.
- Law is the science of what is good or evil.
- Law is established for the benefit of mankind.
- The reason for the law, is the essence of the law.
- When the reason, which is the essence of a law, ceases to exist, the law looses its effect.

- When the law is written on the hearts of mankind, let conscience dictate.
- Ignorance of a law that violates common sense is justifiable.
- An error in a name is nothing when there is certainty as to the person.
- Bad grammar, punctuation & spelling errors do not invalidate a contract or agreement.
- No one is bound to arm or fund their adversary.
- It is lawful to repel force by force, provided it be done with the moderation of blameless defense,
  & not for the purpose of taking revenge, but to ward off injury.
- The law compels no one to do anything which is useless or impossible.
- The law does not notice or care for trifling matters.
- If a law does injury to the innocent, it is void.
- There ought to be an expedient end to all lawsuits.
- Code based legal systems create crime where there is none.
- Crime cannot be fractional, either there is a crime or there is no crime. The Act, Intent & Damage must be present in every crime.
- Tickets & fines for pre-crime are in & of themselves a crime.
- Acts of nature are no fault of others.
- Since no god has been verified present to enter any contract, no person, government, State or Nation can claim sovereignty over the other.
- Sovereignty of State secures slavery & involuntary servitude.
- Usury creates slavery & involuntary servitude.
- No one may be punished for their thoughts.
- Those who do not forbid a crime while they may, potentially sanction it.
- He who makes promises of rewards after life, should be sent ahead to confirm the nonsense.
- Those in the womb are also alive, whether or not it is for their benefit, is not for another to decide.
- Blood, neither a sin nor a crime, can wash away.
- God is love, love is god, a force, not a deity.
- Anyone who claims to speak on behalf of a god, utters hearsay.
- The sum of the law is to love ones neighbor as thyself.

ARTICLE 7. LEGISLATION, TAX, LICENSES & CODES

Article. Section.:7.1 Legislative Powers

All legislative powers shall be vested in the people & implemented through this Constitution. Any change in this Constitution & in law shall be supported by a two-thirds majority vote of all citizens & not just a percentage of those who turn out to vote.

Article. Section.:7.2 No Licenses, Codes Or Ordinances

Licensing, permits, fees, fines tolls & other duties demanded by governments have become nothing short of criminal racketeering, adding huge unnecessary bureaucracy & costs to products & services. No licenses, permits or fees shall be required or demanded by the government other than in the lease of Public-Property. No codes, ordinances or rules shall be enacted anywhere that violate this Constitution.

Responsibility shall lie with the people. Buyer beware. Adults do not need to be treated as children. Those who cause damage are liable for their damage. Acts such as driving without necessary skills, are negligent & shall incur stricter penalties if a negligent driver causes damage. Parents can be liable for damage their children cause. If a builder constructs a building that collapses, the builder is liable. Those who build unsafe or unsightly buildings on public property are liable for their repair or removal & damages. Getting a community involved & participating in building approval, provides a developer more than protection. If a producer claims their product meets certain specifications & the specifications are not met, the producer can be liable for fraud & damages. Anyone causing pollution is responsible for & liable for cleaning it up & restoring the environment. A person that cause significant damage to their neighbor or future generations, is liable. Anyone dealing with or selling to minors, is bound to extra care & is also responsible to the minors parents & society in general. People are responsible for their actions & any impact on neighbors. Act responsibly with respect.

Article. Section.:7.3 No Tax Or Duty

As the people are the government & the people receive Revenue-Share from Public Resources, there is no need for taxation or duty to fund government. There shall be no taxation or duty due other than reasonable lease costs on the Peoples Resources pursuant to the Articles in that regard in this Constitution. To prevent racketeering & profiteering, any fines, tickets or any other charges demanded by any Court, Counties, Provinces, Boards or Associations for offenses or nuisance, shall be payable into the Peopleisim General-Fund. Citizens & Associations who make considerable profits should voluntarily take care of those less fortunate & also contribute to their local, provincial & national infrastructure.

Article. Section.:7.4 No State Marriage License or Registry

No tax advantage or disadvantage being given to married couples eliminates the necessity for any State or People's marriage license or registry. Where a couple wish to merge or share assets & income they should establish an Association defining in detail it's Constitution & terms. Dissolution of the Association shall follow whatever the Associations' Constitution lawfully specifies. Any dissolution of a marriage without any Constitution shall follow the standard due-process under this Constitution. Where people merge assets without any formal contractual terms, the ownership of the assets shall be determined pursuant to standard due-process herein. Where a person wishes to specify inheritance they should register a will & last testament. Associations offering benefits to a spouse must allow the beneficiary to freely name their spouse.

An adult may change their name by a simple change of registration on the Citizen-Services system, however, their given birth name & any past names they register shall remain in the system. Parents governance & care of their children shall be 50/50. A parents access to their children shall never be denied. Any person harming a child may be held criminally liable, including the child's parent/s; the County Board of Directors may appoint a qualified & liable guardian to prosecuted a case in the interests of a child where the evidence of harm to the child is clear & outrageous; Any parent/s found guilty by a jury of outrageously harming their child, may, based on the jury's decision, loose Citizenship, however their Child shall remain a child Citizen & the County Board of Directors & jury shall appoint a suitable guardian under the Board of Directors supervision & mutual liability, to care for the child. Custody disputes that cannot be mutually agreed on by the parents themselves or through mediation, shall follow the standard due-process in this Constitution & be finally decided by a Jury. Where parents decide to live in separate homes, the children should be given a choice & be able to move freely between both parents homes, however, generally parents who separate should have 50/50 access to their children. Responsibility for caring & supporting children should be defined in the Parents Association's Constitution or mutually agreed by parents, if they can not reach an agreement, the support responsibility should generally be 50/50 or according to the percentage with whom the children live or as determined by a Jury.

ARTICLE 8. Citizens & Residents

Article. Section.:8.1 Citizenship & Identity

Any person aged eighteen (18) or older signing their name & thereby taking an oath & affirmation in support of this Universal Peopleisim Constitution, shall be a Citizen. To vote on any matter in a County, Province or Nation, a Citizen must have a registered Homestead in that region. To receive Peopleisim General-Fund Revenue-Share benefits as a Citizen, a Citizen or one of their parents if they are eighteen (18 years) or younger, must practice this Constitution & own a Homestead in a Universal Peopleisim Constitution Nation.

The Identity of Citizens shall be registered with the County & on the Citizen-Services System & shall consist of the following:

- Last Name.
- First Name.
- Other Names.
- Citizen-Services Email.
- Email Secondary (optional).
- Email Tertiary (optional).
- Telephone Primary (optional).
- Telephone Secondary (optional).
- County Name.
- Province Name.
- Nation Name.
- Date of Birth.
- GPS Coordinate of Place of Birth.
- Name at Birth.
- Past Names & dates of name change.
- A photograph updated at least every four years or with major changes in appearance (with the option of setting no general public access).
- A voice recording of the citizen stating their name & another word or short sentence.
- Qualifications (<10,000 characters – optional).
- Chosen practice/s for Citizen-Service.
- Other information the Citizen wishes to voluntarily record for securing their identity (optional).

The citizens photograph & voice recording will be used for Citizen-Services identification & must be kept up to date by the citizen. For added security Citizens may also voluntarily utilize finger prints, retina scans & DNA coding. Identity numbers shall not be used to identify citizens.

To identify an individual the following general sequence should be utilized until identity to the level of security necessary is established: Last Name; First Name; Citizen-Services Email Address; County; Province; Nation; Other Names; Picture; Voice Recording; Birth Date; added optional security such as fingerprints.

Article. Section.:8.2   Registering Citizens Children for Benefits

For children of Citizens to receive benefits the parents must register their children on Citizen-Services after the birth of the child. Each child's registration must be verified by two (2) Directors from the local County Board of Directors & witnessed by two local independent Homesteaded Citizens. Parents who falsely register a child when no child was born, shall loose all Citizenship rights in perpetuity. Parents who fail to properly notify Citizen-Services within a year of their child's death, may loose their Citizenship rights in perpetuity & be required to pay back any overpayment of Revenue Share. Revenue Share for children shall be paid out from the day the child is registered to one month after the child's death. To maintain Citizenship as an adult, in their eighteenth (18) year or older, children of Citizens must also become signatories to this Constitution.

Article. Section.:8.3 Death of a Citizen

Hospitals, morgues, relatives & neighbors are responsible for immediately reporting the death of any Citizen on the Citizen-Services System. Any person who collects the Revenue-Share of a dead person with knowledge of the death, shall loose all Citizenship rights in perpetuity. Revenue Share payment for Citizens shall extend one month after the death of the person to cover burial costs. Any Revenue Share collected over one month after the death of a Citizen, shall be paid back by those who collected it & they shall also be prosecuted for fraud or negligence.

There shall be no death-duty. Citizens are encouraged to register their will & last testament on Citizen-Services. If a deceased person does not have a written will, their inheritance shall vest according to the following order: Fifty percent to their surviving spouse & fifty percent equally to their surviving children (or children's children if their children are deceased), or all to one if the other does not exist; If neither spouse nor any children exist, the inheritance shall vest equally to parents; If parents do not exist, the inheritance shall vest equally to surviving brothers & sisters & if they do not exist; equally to surviving nieces & nephews; If no relatives exist, the inheritance shall vest to the Peopleisim General-Fund. After death, a family will have one year to sell or transfer the dead persons Homestead, after which period any family option to inherit the dead persons Homestead rights shall be lost.

Article. Section.:8.4 Citizen-Service

Each Citizen & Resident over the age of eighteen years (18) shall to the best of their abilities provide the equivalent of thirty two (32) days of eight working hours service each year in service of the people. Citizens aged sixteen (16) & seventeen (17) shall provide ten (10) days Citizen-Service annually. The function, date & time of service shall be appointed by a Board of Directors from the region/s the person lives in. The appointment of higher Board of Directors shall override lower Board of Directors appointments. If not appointed by a Board of Directors, the Citizen or Resident may choose their own function, date & time for Citizen-Service. The allocation & service shall be registered by the Board of Directors and/or Citizen on a Citizen-Services public website for such purpose. Any Citizens will have the opportunity to publicly complement or criticize the service of their fellow Citizens on said website.

The Citizen-Service provided should generally be in line with the skills of the Citizen. Construction workers can assist in maintenance & construction of public properties. Laborers can provide cleanup services of public properties. If not elected & vacancies exist, executives with excellent management skills should be appointed to serve on the Boards of Directors, or appointed to committees of the Boards to assist with management. Experts & analysts can be utilized for the Public-Resource Teams. Auditors can be utilized for auditing the various functions of governance & decisions along with the integrity of voting in other areas. Mediators should offer mediation services in the Courts. Jury duty can be part of Citizen-Service. Counselors can be assigned to help defend those who cannot afford a defense. Doctors can provide their thirty two days service in providing free medical service to the needy. Security professionals can provide service in policing functions. Farmers can care for public lands or assist the needy in establishing vegetable gardens. Each as the Board of Directors determines their best allocation. Each person contributing to the best of their ability, to the good of all. The hours & days of service need not be consecutive. Where necessary, with the Citizen's agreement, a Board of Directors may assign a citizens service for two years concurrent service, which will exempt the Citizen from service in the next year. Citizens may also volunteer for additional Citizen-Service.

Citizens or Residents who cannot provide Citizens-Service because of a serious disability or old age, may apply to a majority of their County Board of Directors for exemption. Citizens who cannot provide Citizen-Service for reasons of travel outside of their region, may apply to a majority of their County Board of Directors or any Board who allocated their service, for a delay of Citizen-Service, or for the provision of a service from a remote location. Where a Citizen reasonably refuses a Board of Directors allocated Citizen-Service, that Citizen must propose a superior use of their time, which if reasonable, must be accepted by the Board/s of Directors.

Failure of any Citizen to provide annual Citizen-Service shall eliminate the Citizen's benefits from Revenue-Share. A Citizen who unreasonably refuses to provide Citizens Service for more than five years, & who refuses to catch up the provision of their services, shall after being found guilty by a Jury for failure to serve, loose their Citizenship & any Citizen rights for ten years & be liable for the equivalent cost of their services not provided over the period they failed to provide Citizen-Service.

Article. Section.:8.5 Non-Citizen Residents

Living in a Peopleisim region is considered a privilege. Residents who are not Citizens shall also be required to provide Citizen-Service & also conform to the terms of this Constitution. If the Resident is not a permanent Resident, the number of days service shall be apportioned according to the percentage of the year they are resident in the region. A Resident who unreasonably refuses to provide Citizens Service for a period of more than five years, & who refuses to catch up the provision of their services, shall after being found guilty by a Jury for failure to serve, be liable for the equivalent cost of their services not provided over the period they failed to provide Citizen-Service & may be evicted from the region.

ARTICLE 9. BOARDS OF DIRECTORS

It is not the intent nor purpose of this Constitution to have a large central government or many meetings of the Boards of Directors. A competently run County, Province & Nation shall establish guidelines, procedures & systems which provide efficient & fair automated, self regulating, balanced management of resources & governance by the people for the people.

The Boards of Directors listed under this Article shall be established to improve efficiency & oversight of peoples based governance. It is the goal of this Constitution that the functions of the Boards of Directors be minimized through the automation provided by Citizen-Services infrastructure & that people based governance rule. All matters before a Board of Directors must be made public & decisions made by any Board of Directors must also be open & accessible to public voting. A majority vote of the people for or against a matter will in all instances rule and/or rescind any Boards vote. The Boards of Directors are subordinate to the people. Only Universal Peopleisim Constitution Citizens Homesteaded in a region may server on any Board.

The concept of a King, Queen, Prime Minister, President or CEO or an Executive Office is specifically not implemented by this Constitution as history has shown Executives & Heads of States invariably become corrupt. Where interaction with other Nations requires a "Head of State" to attend a function, the current Chairman of the International Board of Directors shall assume the role & report back all issues to the People & the Boards of Directors for the people to consider.

Article. Section.:9.1 Election

Candidate Directors shall be proposed & voted for by Citizens to be on various Boards through the Citizen-Services voting system which shall list the proposed candidates for each Board. Any Citizen may propose a Citizen for a position on the various Boards. Candidates will be given equal opportunity for platforms & promotion through the Citizen-Services System. The voting cycle shall be open & Citizens may vote or withdraw their vote for any candidate at any time & will also be able to verify their votes through the system & comment on & rate Directors performance. Citizens may vote for any number of candidates for Boards in their County, Province & Nation. Citizen-Services shall provide Directors email addresses to use exclusively for the Board's business.

Directors who receive the highest number of votes shall be appointed to positions with priority going firstly to Universal Board of Directors, followed International, followed by National, followed by the Advisory Boards, followed by the Provincial, followed by County level Boards of Directors. A Director may however choose to serve on any lower level Board of Directors where they receive sufficient votes or a combination of Boards they are eligible to serve on.

A Director who wishes to serve more than their thirty two days Citizen-Service, may do so voluntarily & they may also canvas for voluntary contributions from Citizens & will be provided with this function through the Citizen-Services System. All Citizen. Contributions made by Citizens to Directors shall be publicly listed on Directors Citizen-Services website. Corporations, Associations & foreign persons or entities, shall be prohibited from making contributions to be used in the promotion or support of any Director.

Article. Section.:9.2   Term of Service

Based on the number of votes the Directors receive, the Citizen-Services System shall dynamically assigned their month & position of service to the various Boards at least one month in advance. Less than a months notice of Service to a Director, may be required with unforeseen circumstances. The Citizen-Services assignment system shall work to ensure the smooth & consistent operation of the Boards of Directors. Directors dates of service shall be scheduled to ensure the Boards consist of a mix & balance of candidates with higher votes throughout the year. Directors shall make every effort to serve on the days they are assigned.

On Synchronous Boards, the first month of a Directors service shall be automatically assigned by the Citizen-Services System one month in advance, & shall count as the Directors annual Citizen-Service. Directors who choose to serve additional months beyond their Citizen-Service, may choose which additional month/s of the year to serve, depending on the availability of positions. Additional months service should be registered a year in advance & may be modified up to two moths prior to service.

On Asynchronous Boards, Directors shall be assigned their start date by Citizen-Services at least one month before service. During service, Directors shall be on call asynchronously throughout the day, day-to-day until their length of service is complete. Directors shall report to Citizen-Services after completing the equivalent of one day (8 hours) service, to be deducted off their thirty two days times eight hours (32 x 8) Citizen-Service & any additional length of time they choose to serve. Two days before a Director leaves the Board the next in line candidate, based on the number of votes received, shall be appointed.

The number of Directors on a Board may at any time be increased or decreased by a majority vote of the Board of Directors or by a majority vote of the citizens in that region. The Board of Directors may also appoint sub-committees from amongst the eligible Citizens in their regions. The assignment of any Citizen to Citizen-Service shall follow the same priorities as the Director Appointments, with the Universal Board of Directors having the highest priority in assignment & the County Boards having the lowest authority of assignment for Citizen-Service.

Vacancies & newly created Directorships resulting from any increase in the number of directors or any absenteeism, shall be filled by the next available person receiving the next highest number of Citizen votes. If insufficient persons receive votes for Directorship Positions on a Board, by a majority vote, higher level Boards of Directors may appoint or remove Citizens for duty on the lower Boards as part of their annual Citizen-Service.

When during service, as a consequence of a significant number of voters withdrawing their vote, a Directors eligibility to serve on a Board based on their number of supporting votes drops below the number of votes the lowest Director on the Board received, the Director shall immediately step down & be replaced by the candidate with the next highest votes.

Article. Section.:9.3 **Boards Of Directors:**

The general functions of the Boards of Directors shall be to monitor the affairs in their region for compliance with this Constitution; To develop & implement plans to address any special needs in their regions & ensure that no person in their region is unfairly taken advantage of; Assign Citizen-Services sensibly without causing undue hardship in the interests of the community; To analyze & monitor security & safety from any internal or external threats to their region & develop & implement plans with the people to address such threats in conformance with this Constitution; To ensure Leases of Public Resources are managed properly & benefit the people & to perform any necessary function in the service of the people to carry out the goals of the Constitution.

In general, Boards of Directors should inspire Citizens in their region to:

- To participate in government providing their Citizens-Service to the best of their ability.
- Vote.
- Conform to the Constitution.
- Properly educate themselves & each other.
- Properly participate in Common Law & the Courts.
- Enhancing the ecology, economy & sustainability of the environment.

There shall be two types of Boards of Directors:

- **Synchronous Boards of Directors:** Directors serve each day of a month. Based on availability, Directors choosing to serve more than one month may choose when to serve the additional months.
- **Asynchronous Boards of Directors:** Directors serve only as necessary, communicating via email, websites & teleconferencing. Service of up to an hour a day for five days a week, representing approximately the full Citizen-Service of thirty two days a year should be the norm. If a Director uses up their Citizen-Service time before the end of year, they may step down & the next available Director takes their position. Based on patterns of service, Citizen-Services may stagger the scheduling of Directors service dates, so as to ensure a mix of Directors with higher vote counts are consistently seated.

The Boards may setup Committees of Citizens to address different functions & tasks & Directors may appoint any number of Citizens serving their Citizen-Service to assist them. The people may also setup their own teams independent of any Board of Directors to perform the functions of the Boards in the interests of the people, who's independent acts shall be verified where necessary, by a majority vote of the people.

Directors shall only utilize their exclusive Board email address for communication of the Boards business which shall be published on blogs setup for the various Boards & Directors, allowing Citizens to follow & audit the Boards & Directors. Two types of communication may be delayed in their publication to the Director & Board Communication Blogs & one type removed:

1. Communication involving the tracking for arrest or expulsion of an extremely dangerous criminal that would prevent capture may be delayed where absolutely necessary from publication on the blog for a maximum of one year, however, typically not more than one week. Such communication shall be released once the criminal is captured.

2. Communication that would clearly undermine the prevention of an imminent violent invasion or violent terrorist attack, may be delayed from publication for a maximum of one year & shall be published when the risk is averted. Let it be noted that the publication & exposure of such threats is often the most powerful means of eliminating the threat.

3. Any communication a Jury classifies a serious libel, or where serious libel is admitted by a perpetrator in mediation, may be removed from any publication.

Article.Section:......9.3.1. **Elders Advisory Board of Directors**

An Asynchronous Elders Board of Directors consisting of twelve (12) concurrent Directors elected at the National level shall be established amongst other identified key functions to:

- Utilizing modern communications methods, without taking up unnecessary time, monitor & provide general guidance, counsel & wisdom to all Boards of Directors;

- Advise the Educational Advisory Board on the best lessons & methods for teaching wisdom.

Article.Section:......9.3.2. **County Board of Directors**

A Synchronous County Board of Directors consisting of twelve (12) concurrent Directors elected at the County level shall be established amongst other identified key functions to:

- Manage the registration & approval of Homestead Rights in the County;
- Properly & fairly manage the allocation of Leases on minor Public-Resources in the County;
- Ensure Leaseholders in their region properly pay their leases into the Peopleisim General-Fund;
- Ensuring the registration of asset ownership in the County on public land is properly conducted;
- Establish Public-Resource Teams & ensure the Teams operate properly & fairly;
- Take care of the needy in their community & ensure no one goes hungry or homeless;
- Ensuring the humane treatment of all beings in the region;
- Ensuring equitable access to public properties & that those who utilize public property properly maintain it;
- Ensure Citizen & Residents have necessary utilities in the region;

- Secure a location/s for Citizen-Services data centers in the County & provide such location & resources if Citizen-Services does not have these resources & facilities in the County;
- Under the guidance of the Communications Advisory Board of Directors, promote & establishing the County communications infrastructure;
- Enforcing eviction of non-compliant Lease Holder's pursuant to the Due-Process in this Constitution;
- Ensuring rights-of-way are open & maintained & ensure there are sufficient & suitable rest-stops for travelers;
- Provide basic assistance as an embassy in effect, to Peopleisim Citizen travelers in trouble;
- In cooperation with the Tourist & Security Advisory Boards, assist in eviction visitors in their region who violate the laws of this Constitution;
- Ensure the people know how to setup Grand Juries & Trial Juries;
- While the people may & should form their own Grand Juries, the County Board of Directors should seat & publish at least one Grand Jury to which people may bring complaints;
- Ensure no gross miscarriage of justice occurs in the County & Courts.

Article.Section:.....9.3.3. Provincial Board of Directors

An Asynchronous Provincial Board of Directors consisting of thirty (30) concurrent Directors elected at the Provincial level shall be established amongst other identified key functions to:

- Oversee the proper conduct of County Boards of Directors in their region;
- Establish Public-Resource Teams & ensure the Teams operate properly & fairly;
- Assign necessary Provincial Citizen-Services sensibly without causing undue hardship in the interests of the Province;
- Properly & fairly manage the allocation of Leases on Medium Public-Resources in the Province;
- Ensure Leaseholders in their region properly pay their leases into the Peopleisim General-Fund;
- Establish Public-Resource Teams & ensure the Teams operate properly & fairly;
- Secure a location/s for Citizen-Services Provincial data center services in the Province & providing such location & resources if Citizen-Services does not have these resources & facilities in the Province;
- Under the guidance of the Communications Advisory Board of Directors, promoting & establishing the Provincial communications infrastructure;
- Ensuring the humane treatment of all beings in the region;
- Ensuring equitable access to public properties & that those who utilize public property properly maintain it;

- Ensure Citizen & Residents have necessary utilities in the region;
- Ensuring rights-of-way are open & maintained & to ensure there are sufficient & suitable rest-stops for travelers;
- In cooperation with the Tourist & Security Advisory Boards, assist in eviction visitors in their region who violate the laws of this Constitution;
- Ensure no gross miscarriage of justice occurs in the Province & Courts;
- Along with the National Board of Directors, govern Badlands in their region.

Article.Section:.....9.3.4. National Board of Directors

An Asynchronous National Board of Directors consisting of fifty (50) concurrent Directors elected at the National level shall be established amongst other identified key functions to:

- Oversee the proper conduct by Provincial Boards of Directors;
- Assign necessary National Citizen-Services sensibly without causing undue hardship in the interests of the Nation;
- Ensure the proper conduct of the Advisory Boards;
- With the vote of a majority of the people, establish or shut down Advisory Boards as necessary in the interests of the people;
- Establish Public-Resource Teams & ensure the Teams operate properly & fairly;
- Properly & fairly manage the allocation of Leases on Major Public-Resources in the Nation;
- Ensure Leaseholders in their region properly pay their leases into the Peopleisim General-Fund;
- Secure a location/s for Citizen-Services National data center services in the Nation & providing such location & resources if Citizen-Services does not have these resources & facilities in the Nation;
- Under the guidance of the Communications Advisory Board of Directors, promoting & establishing the National communications infrastructure;
- In cooperation with the Tourist & Security Advisory Boards, assist in eviction visitors in their region who violate the laws of this Constitution;
- Ensure no gross miscarriage of justice occurs in the Nation & Courts;
- Ensuring the humane treatment of all beings in the region;
- Govern Badlands in their region with the Provincial Boards of Directors.

Article.Section:.....9.3.5. International Board of Directors

An Asynchronous International Board of Directors consisting of no less than twelve (12) concurrent Directors from each Universal Peopleisim Constitution Nation with provisional non-voting positions for up to twelve (12) elected officials from each other Non-Universal Peopleisim Constitution Nation, shall be established amongst other identified key functions to:

- Promoting & assist in the smooth operation & implementation of Universal Peopleisim Constitutions in other Nations;
- Promote a policy of non-interference & ensure peaceful cooperation between Nations;
- Ensure any International dispute is resolved amicably without war or violence;
- Recognizing the United Nations was setup after the bankers League of Nations failed, largely for the purpose of ignoring international banking crime & illegal invasions by the United States & NATO, the International Board of Directors shall be responsible for monitoring & interacting with the United Nations;
- Monitor & help eliminate any International pollution threats;
- Ensure the Citizen-Services Systems provide smooth & fair International banking & trade functions;
- Ensure Revenue-Share is fairly & equitably distributed to each Citizen;
- Under the guidance of the Communications Advisory Boards of Directors, promoting & establishing free or low cost International communications infrastructure;
- In cooperation with the Tourist & Security Advisory Boards, consider visitors civil treatment;
- Ensure no gross miscarriage of justice occurs in any Courts addressing International disputes;
- Ensuring the humane treatment of all beings in the region;
- General oversight of lower level Boards of Directors.

Article.Section:.....9.3.6.   Universal Board of Directors

An Asynchronous Universal Board of Directors consisting of no less than six (6) concurrent Directors from each Universal Peopleisim Constitution Nation & any associated Universal Peopleisim Constitution Planet with provisional non-voting positions for up to six (6) elected officials from each other Non-Universal Peopleisim Constitution Nation and/or associated Planet, shall be established amongst other identified key functions to:

- Promoting & assist in the smooth operation & implementation of Universal Peopleisim Constitutions in new regions;
- Work with Extraterrestrial Civilizations in establishing inter-stellar travel, trade & in the promotion of interstellar peace & prohibition of war;
- Ensure any Universal dispute is resolved amicably without war or violence;
- Under the guidance of the Extraterrestrial & Security Advisory Boards monitor & develop defensive countermeasures to extraterrestrial threats;
- Monitor & help eliminate any space based pollution threats;
- Ensure the Citizen-Services Systems provide smooth & fair Universal banking & trade functions;

- Under the guidance of the Extraterrestrial & Communications Advisory Boards of Directors, monitor any extraterrestrial communications;
- In cooperation with the Extraterrestrial, Tourist & Security Advisory Boards, ensure the civil treatment of any extraterrestrial visitors;
- Ensure no gross miscarriage of justice occurs in any Courts addressing Universal disputes;
- Ensuring the humane treatment of all beings in the region;
- General oversight of lower level Boards of Directors.

Article.Section:.....9.3.7.   Citizen-Services Advisory Board of Directors

An Asynchronous Citizen-Services Board of Directors consisting of no less than twelve (12) concurrent Directors elected at the National level shall be established amongst other identified key functions to:

- Ensure the people are well educated in regard to utilizing Citizen-Services;
- Research & publish effective methods & procedures to ensure the efficient use of Citizen-Services;
- Ensure the Universal, International & National Boards of Directors properly manage the Associations setup to provide Citizen-Services;
- Carry out & publish Audits on the various Citizen-Services Systems;
- Advise the Educational Advisory Board on the best lessons & digital content for teaching Citizens how to effectively use Citizen-Services' Systems.

Article.Section:.....9.3.8.   Due-Process Advisory Board of Directors

An Asynchronous Due-Process Board of Directors consisting of no less than twelve (12) concurrent Directors elected at the National level, five (5) Directors elected at each Provincial level & two (2) Directors elected at the County level shall be established amongst other identified key functions to:

- Ensure the people are well educated in regard to this Constitution, it's Due-Process & Common Law;
- Research & publish effective methods & procedures that ensure efficient, fair & just adjudication;
- Evaluate & ensure the Courts across the nation follow the Constitution's Due-Process & are efficient, just & fair;
- Assist carrying out & in ensuring Jury Duty is properly assigned;
- Assist in establishing Appellate Juries for the various regions;
- Assist as necessary the other Boards of Directors in any legal questions relating to their activities;
- Determine & assist in removing any seriously libelous & untruthful writing on the Boards of Directors websites & blogs pursuant to Due-Process;
- Assist as necessary in prosecuting high-treason cases;

- Advise the Educational Advisory Board on the best lessons & digital content for teaching law, due-process & justice, & take advisory roles as necessary in Courts in the various Counties.

Article.Section:.....9.3.9. Educational Advisory Board of Directors

An Asynchronous Educational Board of Directors consisting of twelve (12) concurrent Directors elected at the National level, five (5) Directors elected at each Provincial level & two (2) Directors elected at the County level shall be established amongst other identified key functions to:

- Research & publish effective education methods, standards & solutions;
- Identify & make available to the people high-quality free education material;
- Make knowledge freely available to all the people so that they can educate themselves;
- As necessary, establish sub-committees of industry experts for specific educational disciplines;
- Cooperate with other Advisory Boards & ensure the education content they recommend is readily available to all people;
- Assist in & ensure a smooth transition of State controlled schools to people controlled universities;
- Assist people, schools, colleges & universities in developing any Educational Lease Proposals;
- Assign Citizen-Service's for the benefit of the people's education.

Article.Section:.....9.3.10. Communications Advisory Board of Directors

An Asynchronous Communications Advisory Board of Directors consisting of twelve (12) concurrent Directors elected at the National level, five (5) Directors elected at each Provincial level & two (2) Directors elected at the County level shall be established amongst other identified key functions to:

- Assist in guiding & in promoting open Internet access across the Nation;
- Manage & reallocate all wireless spectrum in the interests of the people, by the vote of the people, with priority given to open spectrum access (No vendor, owner or employee of any Association or organization that benefits from allocation of spectrum may vote on wireless spectrum allocation);
- As necessary, establish sub-committees for specific communications disciplines;
- Coordinate with the International Telecommunications Unions where necessary;
- Ensure Citizen-Services has access to all necessary networks to provide services to all Citizens;
- Establish & ensure rights-of-way to interconnect public & private communications networks are planned, free & reasonably accessible;

- Establish & manage voluntary funds for the provisioning, installation, maintenance & management of National, Provincial & County terrestrial & wireless open & free Internet;

- Provide guidelines & advice, & where necessary, direct intervention, to prevent network storms, hacking, viruses, snooping or any adverse activity that threatens open, free & non-obtrusive communication by the people & to ensure that the privacy of the people & communications is protected;

- In cooperation with the Security Advisory Board, establish strategic wireless spectrum & communications counter measures to any invading violence of the US Military & NATO's or other terrorist enterprises, while avoiding any interference with commercial GPS spectrum;

- Advise the Educational Advisory Board on the best lessons & digital content for teaching communications technology, & take advisory roles in educational facilities in the various Counties.

Article.Section:.....9.3.11.   Security Advisory Board of Directors

An Asynchronous Security Advisory Board of Directors consisting of no less than twelve (12) concurrent Directors elected at the National level, six (6) Directors elected at each Provincial level & two (2) Directors elected at the County level shall be established amongst other identified key functions to:

- Establish guidelines & procedures for Border Points, including airports, harbors, borders with non Universal Peopleisim nations that ensures safe, relaxed, efficient & secure travel;

- Assign Citizen-Service for managing points of entry in cooperation with the County Boards of Directors with Border Points in their regions;

- Under the Tourist Advisory Board, oversee Citizen sponsorship of foreign visitors & evicting any visitor who becomes a serious risk;

- With the cooperation of County Boards of Directors, assist in tracking down & arresting highly dangerous capital offense criminals pursuant to the due-process & rights of Citizens;

- As necessary, establish sub-committees for specific security concerns or risks;

- Develop & implement strategic defense plans & countermeasures in cooperation with the people & all Boards of Directors for any of the following:
  - False-Flag events;
  - Terrorist attacks;
  - Drone, missile & space weapons attacks;
  - Biological weapons attacks;
  - Nuclear weapons attacks;
  - Conventional & stealth bombing attacks;
  - Battleship & submarine attacks;

- ○ Invasion & occupation by foreign forces, including so-called "peace-keeping" forces;
- With respect of the Geneva Convention, evaluate & develop & implement effective strategy to monitor, evaluate & counter any significant security risks including but not limited to:
  - ○ US Military, NATO, UN or other terrorist invasions;
  - ○ US Military Bases outside of the US;
  - ○ Secret-society infiltration & treason including but not limited to Masonic Gang, Jesuit Gang, Knights of Malta, Mafia, etc.;
  - ○ Establishing an international watch list of known mercenaries & terrorists, such as Blackwater, Mossad, MI5, CIA etc. & prevent risks cause by these terrorists;
  - ○ Evaluate & publish facts of any extraterrestrial threat.
- Cooperate with the Agricultural, Medical, Health & Environmental Advisory Boards in eliminating the GMO threat & any other biological & or chemical weapons threat;
- Research & publish information on False-Flag events, the inside planning of the World Wars & the Jesuit, Masonic, Illuminati & Bankers involvement, to educate the people how to identify & avoid False-Flag events, not be manipulated by them & how to avoid war;
- Identify, expose & eliminate any & all secret-societies & gangs;
- To ensure members of secret-societies who convert to the Peopleisim Citizenship are properly harbored & protected & reveal both the membership, secrets & knowledge of the secret-societies. & to hunt down & prosecute with an iron fist any assassin or terrorist sent by a secret-society to harm any Citizen;
- Identify & coordinate the indictment, arrest & prosecution of bankers who committed & promoted fraud & usury;
- Assemble teams to transfer assets stolen by banking fraud back to the people & Citizen-Services;
- Assist in assembling teams to recover to the people assets belonging to the people that were stolen through unfair mining, banking fraud, war or racketeering;
- Identify & coordinate the indictment, arrest & prosecution of government officials who committed or commit high-treason, grand theft or operated with extreme excess of jurisdiction;
- Establish education programs to make the public fully aware of historical False-Flag events & those behind inciting & profiting from war, recessions & depressions, including but not limited to: Rome's 1st, 2nd, 3rd & 4th Reich's; The Crusades; The Inquisition; The three City-States setup by Rome, namely the Vatican, the inner City-of-London & New Rome a.k.a. Washington D.C.; The Jesuits & Masons roles in wars & control of the courts & government; The Hyksos in Egypt & elsewhere; The

Sumerian Texts; Albert Pike's alleged World War Plans; Formation of the US Federal Reserve Bank & other private Central Banks; Sinking of the Titanic; Sinking of the Lusitania; Reichsag Fire; US Federal Reserve Banks roll in causing the Great Depression & repeated recessions; Pearl Harbor; Operation Paperclip; Sinking of the Ship Liberty; Gulf of Tolkin Incident; Iran Contra Affair; 1993 FBI World Trade Center Bombing; 9/11; London 7/11; Bilderberg Group; Counsel on Foreign Relations; Oklahoma City Bomb; Fukushima; Boston Marathon Bomb & CISPA; The use of the UN & the US Military to invade nations to benefit the bankers; How fractional-reserve fiat-money fraud of banks robs the people; The World Bank & OECD's roll in robing Nations; Bank of International Settlements & other Banks assisting the Nazis steal Gold & other assets; The roll of myths & religion in conflict through the ages; The censorship of extraterrestrial civilizations & life; The use of fluoride, aluminum, mercury, neuro linguistic programing, chemtrails & other methods to dumb-down & hypnotize the public; The Swine-Flu Vaccine global genocide attempt; GMO's impact on health, The pineal glands impact on the state-of-contagiousness; The ongoing theft of gold; etc.

- Ensure counter measures implement peace & do not perpetuate violence;
- Advise the Educational Advisory Board on the best lessons & digital content for teaching security, & as necessary, take advisory roles in educational facilities in the various Counties.

Article.Section:.....9.3.12.   **Transport Advisory Board of Directors**

An Asynchronous Transport Board of Directors consisting of twelve (12) concurrent Directors elected at the National level, six (6) Directors elected at each Provincial level & two (2) Directors elected at the County level shall be established amongst other identified key functions to:

- In cooperation with County Boards of Directors, setup & oversee accounts for airports, harbors & roads, ensuring the funds are not abused & are optimally utilized;
- Assist in managing, building & maintaining roads & right-of-ways across the Nation;
- Ensuring efficient unrestricted travel of Citizens across the Nation;
- Working with the County, Provincial & National Boards of Directors to ensure rights-of-way are safe, open & maintained below the surface, on water, on land, in air & in space;
- Working with County Boards of Directors to ensure there are sufficient suitable rest-stops for travelers;
- Where necessary cooperate & assist the Security Advisory & County Board of Directors in tracking down & arresting dangerous capital offense criminals;

- Where necessary cooperate & assist the Security Advisory & County Board of Directors in evicting visitors who violate the laws of this Constitution;
- As necessary, establish sub-committees for the various transport domains;
- Advise the Educational Advisory Board on the best lessons & digital content for teaching agriculture, & as necessary, take advisory roles in educational facilities in the various Counties.

Article.Section:......9.3.13. **Tourism Advisory Board of Directors**

An Asynchronous Tourism Board of Directors consisting of twelve (12) concurrent Directors elected at the National level, six (6) Directors elected at each Provincial level & two (2) Directors elected at the County level shall be established amongst other identified key functions to:

- Analyze, categorize & promote tourist destinations across the Nation & establish a public rating system for tourist destinations;
- In cooperation with Citizen-Services, establish & manage systems for Citizen sponsorship of foreign visitors & incorporate a contact, help & assistance system for foreign & local tourists;
- Ensure each foreign visitor is educated on the Universal Peopleisim Constitution;
- Ensure efficient enjoyable travel of tourists across the Nation;
- Where necessary cooperate & assist the Security Advisory & County Board of Directors in evicting visitors who violate the laws of this Constitution;
- Advise the Educational Advisory Board on the best lessons & digital content for teaching tourism, & as necessary, take advisory roles in educational facilities in the various Counties.

Article.Section:......9.3.14. **Medical Advisory Board of Directors**

An Asynchronous Medical Board of Directors consisting of twelve (12) concurrent Directors elected at the National level, five (5) Directors elected at each Provincial level & two (2) Directors elected at the County level shall be established amongst other identified key functions to;

- Research & publish effective medicine & medical practice;
- As necessary, establish sub-committees to ensure best-practice medicine for the people;
- Ensure the State controlled hospitals transition smoothly to people-controlled hospitals;
- In cooperation with County Boards, assign medical related Citizen-Service;
- Establish & promote effective free or low-cost people controlled medical insurance options;

- Establish medical review committees & reporting to assist in prosecution of any medical malpractice;
- Eliminate the mind-control foods & treatments such as fluoride, aluminum in deodorant, etc.
- Promote medical benefits of natural remedies, including garlic, anis, hemp oil, etc.
- Advise the Educational Advisory Board on the best lessons & digital content for teaching medicine, & take advisory roles in people's hospitals & medical facilities & in educational facilities in the various Counties.

Article.Section:.....9.3.15. Health Advisory Board of Directors

An Asynchronous Health Board of Directors consisting of twelve (12) concurrent Directors elected at the National level, five (5) Directors elected at each Provincial level & two (2) Directors elected at the County level shall be established amongst other identified key functions to;

- Research & publish effective health science & methods;
- As necessary, establish health sub-committees;
- Assign health related Citizen-Service;
- Establish & promote effective low-cost people controlled health insurance options;
- Ensure the people's sports facilities are properly managed, equipped & available to the people;
- Work with Agricultural Advisory Board to ensure optimal food production for the benefit of the people;
- Eliminate the mind-control foods & treatments such as fluoride, aluminum in deodorant, etc.
- Report on foods, vaccines, medicines & treatments adverse & beneficial effects on people;
- Promote vegetarianism & educate the public on the detrimental effects of meat;
- Promote & educate on living healthy lifestyles amongst the people;
- Advise the Educational Advisory Board on the best lessons & digital content for teaching health science, & take advisory roles in educational facilities in the various Counties.

Article.Section:.....9.3.16. Safety Advisory Board of Directors

An Asynchronous Safety Board of Directors consisting of twelve (12) concurrent Directors elected at the National level, five (5) Directors elected at each Provincial level & two (2) Directors elected at the County level shall be established amongst other identified key functions to:

- Research & provide best-practices & standards for safety professionals;
- As necessary, establish sub-committees for specific safety disciplines, including but not limited to:

- ○ Firefighters;
- ○ Ambulances Associations;
- ○ National Sea Rescue Associations;
- ○ Work Safety Associations;
- ○ Mine Safety Associations;
- ○ Manufacturing Safety Associations;
- ○ Agricultural Safety Associations;
- Work with & ensure the various County Boards of Directors comprehensively coordinate safety strategies & plans & Citizen-Service for safety in each of their regions;
- Advise the Educational Advisory Board on the best lessons & digital content for teaching safety, & take advisory roles in educational facilities & safety Associations in the various Counties.

Article.Section:.....9.3.17.   Environmental Advisory Board of Directors

An Asynchronous Environmental Board of Directors consisting of twelve (12) concurrent Directors elected at the National level, five (5) Directors elected at each Provincial level & two (2) Directors elected at the County level shall be established amongst other identified key functions to:

- Research & publish effective environment monitoring & protection methods & solutions;
- Establish sub-committees as necessary to ensure best-practice environmental management;
- Work with the Mining, Agriculture, Peoples-Parks, Manufacturing & Technology Boards of Directors to promote & ensure the best environmentally friendly practices are promoted by those Advisory Boards;
- Determine methods, initiate & guide projects to recover the planet,s wildlife & nature;
- Assist the People-Parks Advisory Board to ensure proper environmental management of the parks;
- Ensure respect of heritage-object laws & no destruction of trees older than five hundred (500) years.
- Ensure significant archeological sites are preserved;
- Advise the Educational Advisory Board on the best lessons & digital content for teaching environmental science, & take advisory roles in educational facilities in the various Counties.

Article.Section:.....9.3.18.   Agricultural Advisory Board of Directors

An Asynchronous Agricultural Advisory Board of Directors consisting of twelve (12) concurrent Directors made up of five (5) Directors elected from each Province & two (2) Directors elected from each County shall be established amongst other identified key functions to:

- Research & publish best-practices in agriculture;
- Establish sub-committees as necessary to ensure best-practice in agriculture, including encouraging the use of efficient, environmentally friendly & cost effective methods for planting, growing & harvesting;
- Survey the overall cross section of agricultural production to advise farmers on what crops there are likely shortages or excess production of while ensuring there are no monopolistic practices in agriculture to artificially increase the price of produce;
- Ensure ecologically sustainable farming practices are observed;
- Ensure farmers know how to take advantage of the Citizen-Services Trading System;
- Promote organic farming;
- Promote local Homestead agricultural education & programs;
- In cooperation with the Environmental & Medical Advisory Boards, research & publish the dangers of Genetically Modified Food & use of poisons & work to ensure harmful products & practices are eliminated;
- In cooperation with the Environmental & Medical Advisory Boards, research & promotion of the harmful effects of meat production & consumption of meat;
- Advise the Educational Advisory Board on the best lessons & digital content for teaching agriculture, & take advisory roles in educational facilities in the various Counties.

Article.Section:......9.3.19.   Peoples-Park Advisory Board of Directors

An Asynchronous Peoples-Park Advisory Board of Directors consisting of twelve (12) concurrent Directors elected at the National level, five (5) Directors elected at each Provincial level & two (2) Directors elected at the County level shall be established amongst other identified key functions to:

- Research & identify key natural resources in the Nation to be established as Peoples-Parks;
- Ensure Peoples-Parks are properly managed;
- Advise National, Provincial & County Boards of Directors on the establishment of Peoples-Parks;
- Ensure resource extraction operations do not threaten Peoples-Parks;
- Assist regional Boards of Directors in assigning Citizen-Service to take care of Peoples-Parks;
- Oversee & manage any reservation systems & assist in the collection & proper use of use fees for Peoples-Parks;
- Advise the Educational Advisory Board on the best lessons & digital content for teaching on Extractable Resource, & take advisory roles in educational facilities in the various Counties.

Article.Section:.....9.3.20. Extractable Resources Advisory Board of Directors

An Asynchronous Extractable Resources Advisory Board of Directors consisting of twelve (12) concurrent Directors elected at the National level, five (5) Directors elected at each Provincial level & two (2) Directors elected at the County level shall be established amongst other identified key functions to:

- Establish strategies to optimize ecologically sound extraction of natural resources;
- Identify, classify, publish & monitor extractable resources across the Nation, making up-to-date reports to the people;
- Advise National, Provincial & County Boards of Directors on Extractable Resource Leases;
- Working with the Safety Advisory Board, establish & publish safety standards & methods relating to Extractable Resources;
- Working with the Environmental Advisory Board, establish & publish environmental standards & methods relating to Extractable Resources;
- Ensure the resource extractors know how to take advantage of the Citizen-Services Trading System & that all extracted resources are sold through the Citizen-Services system;
- Establish Public Resource Teams to evaluate the former theft of the peoples assets & with other Advisory Boards to determine best methods to recover stolen assets of the people & return the value equally to current & future generations;
- Advise the Educational Advisory Board on the best lessons & digital content for teaching Extractable Resource, & take advisory roles in educational facilities in the various Counties.

Article.Section:.....9.3.21. Technology Advisory Board of Directors

An Asynchronous Technology Advisory Board of Directors consisting of twelve (12) concurrent Directors elected at the National level, five (5) Directors elected at each Provincial level & two (2) Directors elected at the County level shall be established amongst other identified key functions to:

- Research & publish advanced technology solutions & material science to benefit the people;
- Promotion & publication of technological solutions to utilize for the benefit of the planet & life;
- Counter & eliminate the former patent system & any ransom or limitation on access to knowledge, especially Gag-Orders on energy & gravity patents;
- Promote & establish voluntary funds to provide bursaries & sponsorship for promising students;
- Ensure new technology does not threaten the environment, life & the planet;

- Advise the Educational Advisory Board on the best lessons & digital content for teaching Technology & material science, & take advisory roles in educational facilities in the various Counties.

Article.Section:.....9.3.22. Manufacturing Advisory Board of Directors

An Asynchronous Manufacturing Advisory Board of Directors consisting of twelve (12) concurrent Directors elected at the National level, five (5) Directors elected at each Provincial level & two (2) Directors elected at the County level shall be established amongst other identified key functions to:

- Research & publish manufacturing technology, methods, techniques & best-practice;
- Working with the Environmental Advisory Board to ensure manufacturers do not threaten the environment, life & the planet;
- Working with the Safety Advisory Board to ensure best practice is observed in manufacturers;
- Working with the Technology Advisory Board, ensuring the Manufacturers take advantage of the latest technology & material advancements;
- Ensure the Manufacturers know how to take advantage of the Citizen-Services Trading System;
- Advise the Educational Advisory Board on the best lessons & digital content for teaching manufacturing technology, & take advisory roles in educational facilities in the various Counties.

Article.Section:.....9.3.23. Extraterrestrial Advisory Board of Directors

An Asynchronous Extraterrestrial Advisory Board of Directors consisting of twelve (12) concurrent Directors elected at the National level, five (5) Directors elected at each Provincial level & two (2) Directors elected at the County level shall be established amongst other identified key functions to:

- Research & publish credible reputable verifiable sources of information on extraterrestrial civilizations & life such as The Disclosure Project;
- Help eliminate the centuries of censorship of extraterrestrial life & civilization;
- Promote a peaceful non-fear based understanding of extraterrestrial beings;
- Research & publish information on extraterrestrial anti-gravity technologies & vehicles;
- Ensure extraterrestrial technology does not threaten the environment, life & the planet;
- Advise the Educational Advisory Board on the best lessons & digital content for teaching about extraterrestrial civilizations, & take advisory roles in educational facilities in the various Counties.

Article.Section:.....9.3.24. **Energy Advisory Board of Directors**

An Asynchronous Energy Advisory Board of Directors consisting of twelve (12) concurrent Directors elected at the National level, five (5) Directors elected at each Provincial level & two (2) Directors elected at the County level shall be established amongst other identified key functions to:

- Research & publish free-energy technology solutions;
- Identify & promote the best free-energy technology;
- Convert all the former State or pseudo-State energy production to distributed people controlled energy production;
- Ensure Citizen & Residents have necessary utilities in the region;
- Establish plans for phasing out oil based vehicles;
- Safely eliminate all nuclear power plants;
- In cooperation with the Technology, Manufacturing & Transport Advisory Boards, research & publish anti-gravity technologies & vehicles;
- Ensure new technology does not threaten the environment, life & the planet;
- Advise the Educational Advisory Board on the best lessons & digital content for teaching about energy technologies, & take advisory roles in educational facilities in the various Counties.

Article.Section:.....9.3.25. **Badlands Advisory Board of Directors**

An Asynchronous Badlands Advisory Board of Directors consisting of no less than twelve (12) concurrent Directors elected at the National level, & in regions with Badlands four (4) Directors elected at the Provincial level, three (3) Directors at the County level, shall be established amongst other identified key functions to:

- Monitor the effectiveness of Badlands regions;
- Study & publish effective methods to prevent crime & civilize criminals;
- Advise the National & Provincial Boards of Directors on the implementation & management of Badlands regions;
- Publish open reports on Badlands regions highlighting success, failure & any abuse, while respecting security;
- Advise the Educational Advisory Board on the best lessons & digital content for teaching morals to prevent crime, & take advisory roles in educational facilities in the various Counties.

Article.Section:.....9.3.26. **Restitution Advisory Board of Directors**

An Asynchronous Restitution Advisory Board of Directors consisting of no less than twelve four (12) concurrent Directors elected at the National level, six (6) Directors elected at each Provincial level & three (4) Directors elected at the County level shall be established amongst other identified key functions to:

- Work with the Citizen-Services Bank to establish software & algorithms to calculate the value fiat-currencies in grams of gold (gg) at specific dates for use in Restitution calculations;

- Where necessary, assist & oversee Public-Resource Teams & ensure all their findings & calculations are published on the relative public websites;
- Ensure Public-Resource Teams operate with complete integrity & publish all relevant findings;
- Assist the Security Advisory Board & any Public-Resource recovery team in any way they can to recover public-assets to the people;
- Publish restitution progress, information & figures.

Article. Section.:9.4 Retarded Action

The purpose of the Boards of Directors is to provide efficiency in governance & to promote & not limit the peoples power. All matters decided by a Boards of Directors, including approval of Leases & Homestead allocations, shall also be constantly listed for vote on the relevant Board of Directors websites & the option given to Citizens to also vote on the matters, shall not be removed for the duration of any lease. A quarter of Citizens votes from a region in opposition to a Board of Directors decision, will rescind the Board of Directors decision & require unanimous vote by the Board to re-institute the decision. A majority of Citizens votes from the region shall in all instances counter any decision made by any Board of Directors & approve or deny the matter.

Article. Section.:9.5 Indemnification

By a majority vote of a Board of Directors, indemnification & advance payment of expenses may be granted to Directors & Agents, including Jurors, against all reasonable expenses actually & necessarily incurred by them in connection with the defense of any litigation to which they may have been made a party because they were acting in the interest of the people. The individual shall have no right to reimbursement, however, in relation to matters as to which they have been adjudged liable for gross negligence or misconduct in the performance of their duties, or where they were derelict in the performance of their duty by reason of willful misconduct, bad faith, gross negligence or reckless disregard of the duties of their office or position. The right to indemnity for expenses shall also apply to the expenses of suits settled in mediation.

Article. Section.:9.6 Meetings of the Boards

Meetings of the Boards of Directors for any purpose may be held at reasonable times & places either Synchronously or Asynchronously. All Board meetings & communications of Directors shall be recorded, & published live where possible, & published with transcripts as soon as possible on the Board of Directors website.

The Chairman of each Board shall be present at all meetings of the Boards & copied on all communications between Directors, if the Chairman of the Board is unable to attend any meeting, he shall appoint in writing for each meeting a Stand-in-Chairman for such specific purposes.

Within what is reasonable & practicable, without causing any disruption, citizens may attend & monitor all meetings & communications of the Boards of Directors.

Article. Section.:9.7   <u>Notice of Synchronous Meetings of the Boards</u>

Notice of synchronous meetings of the Boards of Directors shall be given in writing via email to all Directors & published on the relative website not less than:

- International Board of Directors Meetings: fourteen (14) days prior to the meeting.
- National Board of Directors Meetings: ten (10) days prior to the meeting.
- Provincial Board of Directors Meetings: seven (7) days prior to the meeting.
- County Board of Directors Meetings: five (5) days prior to the meeting.

Article. Section.:9.8   <u>Veto.</u>

The Chairman of a Board shall have veto powers on any matter voted on by the Board of Directors. The invocation of such a veto shall bring the matter to the direct attention & vote of the Citizens in accordance with the Citizens voting rights.

Article. Section.:9.9   <u>Use Of Communications Equipment</u>

Meetings of the Board of Directors & Committees of the Board may be effectuated by means of communications equipment that allows all persons to either hear or read all input, & identify participants making the input. Participation by such means constitutes presence in person at the meeting.

ARTICLE 10. Voting, Notices, Meetings & Actions of Boards & Citizens

Peopleisim implements real-time democratic voting. There is no election cycle. Matters are registered for vote, once the matter receives sufficient votes it is enacted.

Article. Section.:10.1   <u>Registering Voting Matters</u>

A quarter or more of the members of any Board of Directors may register any matter for voting in their region. Fifty (50) Citizens may register a matter for voting at the County level; one thousand (1000) Citizens at the Provincial level & five thousand (5,000) Citizens at the National level. Any website may be used to promote ideas & collect the required number of voters to register a matter for voting. Following proof of support by the promoter of the matter, it will be tabled on the relevant County, Province or National website & their supporters must formally register their support for registering the matter to vote within five days of the matter being tabled. Once registered, these matters will be open to gather votes on the relevant County, Provincial or National websites. If a matter fails to obtain the necessary number of votes after being open for vote for two years, it shall be removed.

Article. Section.:10.2   Publication of Voting Matters & Comments

Once registered, matters open for vote shall be published on the regional websites providing relevant information relating to the matter. Each matter will have open comment sections that may be sorted & ranked based on Citizens supporting, opposing or abstaining on the matter, along with the voters name & any related qualification of the Citizen voting & commenting. The number of views & ratings by readers shall also be listed. Libel & foul language shall be prohibited. The comment section shall also cater for setting aside spam or abuse, however, said comments & spam shall also be publicly listed in a spam section linked to the voting matter.

Article. Section.:10.3   Notice Of Citizen Voting Matters

A Notice via email of any matter tabled for citizen vote shall be sent to each Citizen eligible to vote on the matter within five days of the matter being registered. Said Notice shall include a categorized title of the voting matter with a link to the matters web-page & any opposing web-page/s & shall not contain more than five hundred characters describing the matter by those tabling the matter for vote. A five hundred or less character description opposing the mater, shall also be included in the Notice by any organized opposition that receives in opposition the prerequisite number of votes necessary to register the matter. The regions website shall list all Notices, describing, promoting & opposing the matter, which should also provide links to other relevant web pages that received a prerequisite number of "likes" from voters for registering a matter.

Article. Section.:10.4   Right to Vote

Only Citizens with Homesteads, or Citizens registered & confirmed as permanently living at a Homestead by the Homestead Owner, in the region the matter is applied to, may vote. The right of Citizens eligible to vote shall not be restricted. All votes shall be made & recorded on-line through official regional sites setup for voting. When the requisite majority of Directors and/or Citizens vote in support of a matter, the matter shall be approved & enacted. In all cases, a majority of the people shall overrule any Board of Directors votes. If it appears that a majority of Citizens are likely to vote in opposition to a measure when a majority of a Board of Directors have approved it, the approval shall be delayed a further two weeks to allow Citizens to vote on the matter. Any Citizen found guilty by a jury of selling or trading their vote, shall cease to be a Citizen.

Article. Section.:10.5   Registration of Votes

Where possible, with each vote a picture of the person voting at the time of the vote shall be registered. In all cases the voters official email address including any routing & time stamping on the vote shall be registered. An email confirmation shall be sent to each citizen confirming the details of their vote & their vote shall be registered & publicly viewable on the relative voting site. Citizens may change their vote at any time. Citizen-Services shall be responsible for providing the voting systems, services, verification & vote integrity checks including public audits of the votes. Public voting & information stations shall also be provided by Citizen-Services at convenient locations for access by people unable to access on-line voting.

Article. Section.:10.6 <u>No Secrecy</u>

There shall be no secret or hidden meaning nor intent in words or sentences, the purpose & intent of a word or sentence should be clear & obvious & carry the meaning as understood by the common person.

To prevent fraud in vote counting & verification, there will be no secrecy in voting. A person is publicly accountable for what & who they vote for.

Article. Section.:10.7 <u>Quorum</u>

For a matter to be approved a quorum is necessary. A quorum is reached when more than half of all Directors on a Board or more than half the citizens from the region in which the vote is being counted, vote in favor of a matter, unless by express provision of this Constitution a specific matter requires a different vote.

In all voting matters the specified percentage of each & every eligible voter from a region entitled to vote shall be considered, & not just a count of those who turn out to vote for or against a matter.

Article. Section.:10.8 <u>Abstention Vote</u>

In all voting matters an Abstention Vote option must be provided for expressing no interest in the matter. Abstention Votes shall be counted for removing the matter from the ballot & added to opposing votes. Where more than half a region's voters vote for an Abstention Vote on a matter, the matter shall not be listed again for voting on for a period of three (3) years.

Article. Section.:10.9 <u>Waiver</u>

Whenever a notice is required, the person or persons entitled to such notice, may choose in writing to set aside the need for the notice.

ARTICLE 11. <u>R</u>EGIONS & <u>B</u>OUNDARIES
OF <u>U</u>NIVERSAL <u>E</u>ARTH

National Boundaries have been artificially created, generally by ruling classes starting wars to gain control to benefit themselves personally & to steal Natural Resources. The primary focus of National boundaries is generally to divide & conquer. National Boundaries, in effect are foreign to the concepts of Peopleisim. It is the divisions in societies that cause civilization to fail. A civilized society does not force boundaries other than respect for a persons Homestead & the right to travel & do business fairly without hassles & to enjoy the beauty of nature & the planet. In order to create effective management, Peopleisim implements six regions, the Homestead, County, Province, Nation, Planet & Universe. The primary active governance is at the County Level. At the National level, Peopleisim Nations cooperate to eliminate war & promote cooperation.

Article. Section.:11.1 Citizen Homestead

Each citizen over the age of eighteen (18) shall be entitled to own up to two thousand square meters (2,000m²) of land in no more than two parcels as their Homestead. Naturally in regions where there is limited space, Homesteads will be smaller. Multistory residential building owners may divide their Homestead land ownership on the land footprint of the buildings property.

There shall be no taxation, duties or any fees levied against a Citizens' Homestead. A Citizens Homestead may not be taken from them except according to any specific clause in this Constitution.

Citizens may build what they choose on their Homestead without permits, licenses or any other demands, save what genuinely amounts to an unreasonable pollution threat.

No person may enter a Homestead without the permission of the owner, save those issued a lawful warrant granting access in conformance to this Constitution's specific clauses.

Applications for, & registration of Citizen Homesteads shall be fairly managed & recorded by the County Board of Directors on the Citizen-Services system, respecting the preservation of agricultural land, mining land, leased land, People's Parks, the commons & rights-of-way. Oversight from Provincial & National Boards of Directors shall ensure fair allocation.

Any Citizen wishing to establish a Homestead in a County, must file an application on the Citizens-Services system website for that County. Subject to the availability of land suitable for Homesteads, with a consecutive two-month majority vote the County Board of Directors will reasonably allocate a suitable Homestead site, preferably where the applicant requests, however, respecting no degradation of Peoples-Parks, agricultural land, key ecological or key economic land, or rights-of-way, & taking into account existing neighbors desires, & if any of the following conditions are met:

- The Citizen lawfully owns the home or building at the establishment of this Constitution.
- The adult Citizen is a child of a parent with a Homestead in the County.
- A person is a member of an indigenous people displaced from the region.
- The Citizen applying has been resident in the County for total of ten (10) cumulative years.
- One hundred (100) or more Citizens with Homesteads in the County vote to sponsor a newcomer.
- A two-month majority of the County Board of Directors approves the new Citizen Homestead application.

At their discretion, a majority of the Provincial & National Board of Directors may order a County Board of Directors to take measures to properly accommodate a Citizens Homestead application.

Citizens Homesteads shall be acquired on a first-come first-serve basis & may also be bequeathed, surrendered to the people, transferred or sold; If the sale is not for another Citizens Homestead, the buyer will also need to establish a land lease agreement with the County Board of Directors pursuant to the Lease terms of this Constitution. Allowing for a maximum of six (6) months to move to a new Homestead, Citizens must ensure their former Homestead is no longer registered in their name; any Citizen who attempts to hold more than two thousand square meters as their Homestead shall by the vote of a majority of any Board of Directors in the region/s loose their Homestead rights for five (5) years & entirely for a third offense.

Where a Homestead lies on or in the path of an important right-of-way, Extractable Resource / mine or major public project, either a majority of the people from the County or Province may vote & contribute to pay for moving of the Citizens Homestead to a similar or superior site, or a Replacement Lease Agreement must cover the moving costs.

Water from the land necessary for running a Homestead & its agricultural needs, shall be freely available to the Homestead owner, excess water entering the land must be allowed to continue on down its natural course. Where there is no water available on a Homestead site, the Homesteader must be given reasonable access by neighbors to other nearby water-sources.

It is a Citizens duty to ensure that the land on which they establish their Homestead is kept as they found it or is improved. Polluting a Homestead is prohibited & shall be enforced reasonably by the County Board of Directors. While chemical pollution is the primary concern, said pollution can also be of a visual or sound nature. When one hundred (100) or more Citizens from the County object in writing to significant pollution on or from a Homestead in their County, the County Board of Directors shall issue a Notice signed by a majority of the Directors, ordering the Citizen to cleanup the pollution within a reasonable period, generally one year. If the offending Homestead is not cleaned within the reasonable time, with a majority vote of the County Board of Directors, a necessary proportion of the Citizens share of Peopleisim General-Fund distribution may be allocated to paying for cleaning up the pollution according to the County Board of Directors instructions. If the funds are not sufficient to cleanup the pollution, pursuant to the due-process prescribed herein, the Homesteader may be charged with criminal negligence & if found guilty, the Jury may in their judgment determine if the Citizen should be expelled from their Homestead.

Except in the case where a Citizens registers with a County Board of Directors for extended travel, where land registered as a Citizen's Homestead is not occupied at all by the Citizen through a seven (7) year period, the land shall become public land, however not without just compensation for the buildings & improvements the owner added to the property.

Squatting on the land shall be prohibited. People may not simply move in on public land, they must apply to a County Board of Directors to obtain Homestead rights, or lease the land & obtain formal written permission from the County Board of Directors. The County, Provincial, National & International Boards of Directors shall establish Resource Teams who's responsibility is to identify land suitable for Indigents, Squatters & Refugees & assist those unfortunate enough to be so compromised in establishing decent futures on Homesteads or land allocated to their recovery.

Article. Section.:11.2 County

The County Board of Directors shall form the primary seat of governance & shall be responsible for identifying, allocating & registering Homesteads & other functions defined in the Board of Directors Article of this Constitution.

At the establishment of this Constitution, existing Counties or Wards shall be recognized; when a majority of adults in these Counties or Wards become signatories to this Constitution, that County or Ward shall be declared a County under this Universal Peopleisim Constitution.

If a majority of adult Citizens in each of two existing Counties vote to enjoin their neighboring Counties, the two Counties shall become one.

A minimum of five hundred (500) to a maximum of one hundred thousand (100,000) adult Citizens, living in a contiguous region on a minimum of one square kilometer (1 km²) to a maximum of twenty five thousand square kilometers (25,000 km²), all in full agreement with the people in that contiguous region, may establish their own new County in conformance to this Constitution. In high-density city areas, the minimal limitations on area may be calculated taking into account multistory surface area. Counties should follow natural geographic formations & must form contiguous areas, which may in the case of islands, incorporate a group of islands.

Public Land is not open for random use, but rather assigned for specific public use or leased for specific functions by the County Board of Directors & the Citizens of the County. In order to ensure the land is taken care of, County Boards of Directors may assign Citizen & Resident guardians of the land to ensure the assigned function of the land is respected. While animals may roam freely across public land, the general public shall generally be restricted to public rights-of-way which may also include general roaming regions for hiking & other activities. Counties shall ensure sufficient & suitable rights-of-way are provided to access Homesteads, all reasonably significant locations & bordering Counties. Citizens in a County are responsible for policing & taking care of their County.

While there shall be no prohibition of citizens running business from their Homestead, the County Boards of Directors should map out commercial & industrial regions where the land is best leased for commercial purposes & not for homesteads. The city center, industrial districts & mines should be set aside for commercial zoning. Residential areas should be set for homesteading. Agricultural land should be set for agricultural leases allowing for non-arable regions within the agricultural area to be utilized for homesteads.

Article. Section.:11.3 Provincial

A Province (also referred to as a State) shall consist of at least four contiguous Counties or as it was defined at the formation of this Constitution. New Provinces may be formed with the majority vote of Citizens in each of four or more contiguous Counties, so long as there remains at least four Counties in the original Province. Provinces may merge with other contiguous Provinces with a majority vote of the people in each Province. The Provincial Board of Directors shall be responsible for identifying, allocating & registering Counties on the Citizen-Services Registry & other functions defined in Board of Directors Article of this Constitution.

Article. Section.:11.4   National

A Nation may consist of any number of consensual Provinces or as defined at the formation of this Constitution. New Nations may be formed with the majority vote of Citizens in one or more Provinces. Nations may merge with other contiguous Nations with a majority vote of the people in each Nation. The National Board of Directors shall be responsible for identifying, allocating & registering Provinces on the Citizen-Services Registry & other functions defined in Board of Directors Article of this Constitution.

Article. Section.:11.5   Air

The airspace above the land must be respected within reasonable safe unobtrusive limits from a safety, noise & pollution perspective. Any person or Association causing serious pollution damage that is carried by air to neighboring properties can be criminally liable & is not only responsible for ceasing & desisting, but also for any necessary cleanup. Prosecution of polluters shall follow the due process prescribed herein & may be instituted reasonably by any affected Citizen.

Flight paths should attempt to follow the least obtrusive path with practical & reasonable limits. As anti-gravity vehicles become the norm for travel, three dimensional rights-of-way must be established to ensure safe unencumbered travel with ease of access to necessary points, including Homesteads & leased property & open commons.

Article. Section.:11.6   Water

Bodies of water larger than one hundred thousand (100,000 l) liters shall be considered the people's natural resources & shall not be polluted. Those responsible for causing significant pollution in or on the land which is washed into the sea, waterways, rivers, dams or ponds, shall be held criminally liable for damage & responsible for cleanup or the costs thereof in addition to putative damages. Waterways which are utilized as rights-of-way, shall not be restricted.

The oceans shall be considered common territory & shall extend to the high-water mark of the coastline to the center of the ocean between a neighboring Nation. Public beach access shall not be restricted up to the high-water mark.

Over the 1800's, 1900's & early 2000's, the oceans have been subject to the tragedy of the commons. Greedy fisheries have wiped out most of the life in the oceans. The extent & violence of this damage is so extreme that ceasing & desisting all commercial fishing, save properly managed farms, is the only option. As this Constitution provides Homesteads & income for Citizens, no extreme hardship is caused by such protective measures. The commercial fisheries who have caused the devastation need to be prosecuted for their crimes.

There shall be no dumping of waste in the ocean. Those responsible for causing significant pollution in the ocean or on the land which is washed into the ocean, shall be held criminally liable for damage & responsible for cleanup or the costs thereof in addition to putative damages. Responsibility for cleaning up damage caused by pollution, shall be shared by those responsible for using, selling, marketing & manufacturing the product or action that caused the pollution, according to their relative negligence & ability to pay.

Any mining of minerals in or below the ocean shall be subject to lease contracts governed by the International Board of Directors & the proceeds shall be shared equally amongst the Citizens of all Universal Peopleisim Constitution Nations. Any mining or agricultural operation in the ocean shall strictly conform to ecological & environmental standards which do not in any way damage or put at reasonable risk life & the ecology of the oceans, while conforming to all the other terms of the lease of Natural Resources. Prosecution of polluters shall follow the due process prescribed herein & may be instituted reasonably by any Citizen or Association of Citizens.

Article. Section.:11.7   Earth

As a beautiful planet the earth must be protected. This Universal Peopleisim Constitution is established to protect & properly manage the planet Earth. When a majority of people on Earth have signed & adopted this Constitution, it shall be declared the law of the planet Earth.

Those responsible for causing significant pollution on Earth shall be held criminally liable for the damage & responsible for cleanup or the costs thereof in addition to putative damages.

Article. Section.:11.8   Space

Access to space shall not be prohibited. No atomic weapons shall be taken into space. Those engaging in space flight shall be responsible for any significant pollution they cause, & shall be held criminally liable for damage & responsible for cleanup or the costs thereof in addition to putative damages.

Article. Section.:11.9   The Badlands

The Prison & Jail systems of the Old World Order that calls itself the New World Order have not been effective, while their prison industrial complex, is in & of itself a heinous criminal act.

How a person is raised as a child in addition to the behavior of leaders, has a significant effect on how they turn out as adults. Communities should take an active roll in ensuring people are raised well in their County. Allowing children to play violent games including computer games, or watch movies that glorify violence, will teach violence as will any other promotion or glorification of violence, such as that which is so readily promoted on mainstream media & by Hollywood. Only one child needs to go bad to ruin the lives of many innocent people in a community.

When a person is found guilty of a heinous crime the option of sending them back to the County where they were predominantly raised as a child or influenced into crime, to be taken under the agreed supervision of the Board of Directors from that County, should be considered by the Jury. The family & community where a child is raised, can be largely responsible for how that person turns out.

On occasions where individuals commit such heinous crimes that they are a serious threat to society & are unlikely to reform to anywhere close to acceptable behavior, or if their crime was so horrific that the people in the County who were victims of the crime deserve their liberty from association, if the victims so choose, the criminal may be expelled where: A jury rules that a person may be expelled from a County, & the Board of Directors of that County votes unanimously to expel the criminal; or if more than half the Citizens of that County vote to expel a criminal found guilty of a heinous crime. In such cases, the criminal shall be excluded from Homestead, Lease or Travel rights in that County & the criminal shall be sent back & restricted to the County where they were predominately raised as a Child for a reasonable length of time determined by the Jury. If a majority of the Board of Directors or more than a quarter of the Citizens of the County where the criminal was predominantly raised as a child, vote to not receive the criminal back into their County where they will be responsible for properly rehabilitating the criminal to civilized behavior, the criminal shall be sent to the Badlands. The reason a person committed crime must always be considered when metering out punishment with the goal of removing or finding a remedy for the reasons & causes.

The purpose of the Badlands is to provide a location no one else wants, where criminals are forced to come to terms with themselves & nature, to learn respect, humility, care & above all love. The Badlands should humiliate bad behavior & not to create humiliation; the purpose is to break down what is bad, & build up what is good with dignity & respect. The propensity of humans to become abusive when placed in strict authority of other people, must be carefully considered when setting up & managing the Badlands. Criminals shall not be allowed any weapons in the Badlands. No animal may be killed or eaten in the Badlands. Criminals sent to the Badlands shall not be eligible to vote on any matter outside the Badlands. Respecting security, with the Provincial or National Board of Directors approval, any person may enter & leave the Badlands according to the Board of Directors specific instructions & limitations, & no independent reporters or investigators shall be prohibited from investigating & reporting on the efficiency or inefficiency or problems in Badlands regions.

The following types of crimes, where the intent is irrefutable & premeditated, the act atrocious, & the damage devastating, apply to the Badlands: Murder; Rape; Genocide; Extreme excess-of jurisdiction by judges; Committing serous crimes under the color of law by politicians, police, prosecutors & lawyers; drug pushers & hookers who enslave & destroy the lives of others; Bankers who use fiat-money to steal & destroy people's lives.

With the guidance of the Badlands Advisory Board, the Provincial & National Board of Directors shall be responsible for governing any Badlands in their regions. The Badlands shall be desolate locations that are appropriately enclosed or fenced where necessary & the guilty criminal shall be granted a homestead within the Badlands. Sufficient water to survive & grow vegetables must be reasonably available or made available. The cost of setting up the Badlands shall be born by the guilty party, which may also come from their share of the Peopleisim General-Fund. If the criminal cannot afford to pay for their cost of the Badlands, the cost shall be covered by donations or by the County who expelled the criminal to the Badlands.

ARTICLE 12. LEASING PEOPLES RESOURCES & RECOGNITION OF PRIVATE ASSETS

Aside from Citizens Homesteads & persons or Association Assets, the Resources & Assets on the planet, shall belong equally to the Citizens, including the mineral resources, land, rights-of-way, public buildings, public utilities, agricultural resources, water, radio spectrum etc. The natural resources have always belonged to the people, simply because a former government who was controlled by a criminal cartel & greed authorized the theft of the peoples assets does not make that theft just. In Nazi Germany everything Hitler did was lawful because he made the law. The theft of the peoples assets shall be recovered to the people equally for the current & future generations. Any major natural resource below a Homestead, shall also belong equally to the citizens. No living being with a beating heart shall be listed as or considered a Natural Resource. Over the course of a lease, save for extracted resources fairly & properly paid for, it is the duty of a Lessee to ensure that the land they lease is the same as it was when they first leased it or improved. Polluting of the land, water & air shall be strictly prohibited & enforced by the various Boards of Directors & the people. The lease of & the restitution of former owners for resources & assets transferred to the public through the transition to this Constitution, including the mining, farming & utilization of Public-Resources & Assets, shall be governed by the National, Provincial & County Boards of Directors & the people according to the following terms:

Article. Section.:12.1 Classification Of Public-Resources & Assets

Public-Resources shall be valued according to their equivalence in grams or kilograms of gold (gG or kgG):

- **Minor Public-Resources:** valued below the equivalent value of one hundred kilograms of gold (100 kgG) shall be managed by the County Board of Directors.

- **Medium Public-Resources:** valued at the equivalent of value of between one hundred kilograms of gold (100 kgG) & two thousand kilograms of gold (2,000 kgG) shall be managed by the Provincial & County Boards of Directors.

- **Major Public-Resources:** valued at the equivalent of value of over two thousand kilograms of gold (over 2,000 kgG) shall be managed by the National, Provincial & County Boards of Directors.

By a majority vote of the people or by a unanimous consecutive five-month (5) vote of the National Board of Directors, the value range of these classifications may be modified.

Article. Section.:12.2   Public-Resource Teams

Each Board of Directors shall establish Public-Resource Teams to competently & fairly establish the value of resources & assets in their region, & ensure fair & reasonable Lease terms on the Resources provide maximum profit & returns to the people. Each Public-Resource Team setup by the Boards of Directors shall consist of the following number of Directors responsible for the Public-Resource & complemented with a sufficient number of competent Citizens with expertise in the type of asset or resource:

- Major Public-Resource Teams shall consist of teams setup by all three of the National, Provincial & County Boards of Directors, with nine or more Directors consisting of three or more Directors from each of the Boards on the team.
- Medium Public-Resource Teams shall consist of teams setup by both the Provincial & County Boards of Directors, with six or more Directors consisting of three or more Directors from each Board on the team.
- Minor Public-Resources Teams shall consist of teams setup by the County Board of Directors consisting of three or more Directors on each team.

Independent Public Resource Teams may also be set by the people, independent of any Board of Directors, to evaluate Public-Resources in any region. Where an independent Public Resource Team is set up by the people, their findings shall be clearly & fully published alongside the findings of any Public Resource Team set up by a Board of Directors for the same or effectively the same resource.

If a resource crosses County, Province or National regions, three Directors from each of the Boards regions shall be put on the Resource Team. Professionals serving their Citizens-Service on Resource Teams may be drafted from neighboring Counties & Provinces to ensure the integrity & fairness of the evaluation & establishment of Lease terms. In all instances, the members of Pubic Resource Teams may have no personal interest nor receive any direct return whatsoever from the evaluation, establishment or approval of a Lease Proposal. All information, rational & decisions, relating to the Resource Teams evaluation & lease recommendations & names of the team shall be public & published on the relevant Board of Directors website. The Resource Teams shall be responsible for the following functions:

- Identification, registration & valuation of resources & assets in their region;
- The promotion of Public-Resources in their region;

- Selection & appointment of Citizens to Citizen-Service for assisting the Public Resource Team;
- The establishment, promotion & negotiation of Leases Agreements on Resources in their region;
- Calculation of Restitution for land & property turned over to the public;
- Calculation of compensation to former lease holders for any assets contributed, & improvements made by the former owner that remain on the land following a Replacement Lease;
- Establishing maintenance & improvement plans for the Public-Resources & the amount & schedule of lease payments to pay for said maintenance & improvements, & the amount & schedule of the lease payments to be contributed to the General-Fund;
- Ensuring all this information is public & published on the relative Board of Directors website.

Where it becomes completely necessary to maintain a Citizen expert or Director on a Resource Team beyond their annual thirty two days Citizen-Service, with a majority of the applicable Board of Directors ongoing approval, reasonable compensation of the expert may be derived from the lease of the resource, however, in no instance should said compensation exceed one quarter of the public returns from the lease.

Article. Section.:12.3   Open Market On Public-Resources

Revenue from the Lease of Public-Resources shall be distributed equitably to all Citizens through the Peopleisim General-Fund pursuant to the terms in this Constitution. A system which optimizes the return for the people while eliminating corruption that personally profits individuals at the expense of the people, is necessary. Consequentially, the Peopleisim Public-Resource Lease process is completely open, allowing the people to follow & observe all the details of leases, & allowing anyone who can provide a superior return to the people, to replace any existing lease, except where a lease is given as restitution for private property turned over to the public which may have a maximum term of up to one hundred (100) years.

The People & Boards of Directors may solicit Lease Proposals for Resources in their regions. Standard terms & guidelines for Lease Proposals may be established by the National, Provincial & County Boards of Directors & implemented & managed by the Boards & the People. Standard forms for submitting Lease Proposals shall be provided on the Citizen-Services System. Lease Proposals made by Citizens or Associations shall be listed up to the point they are approved, but not for more than four years.

Article. Section.:12.4   Lease Proposals

Any Citizen, or Association wholly owned by Citizens may propose or bid on the Lease of Public-Resources. All proposals, bids & Lease awards of Public-Resources shall be published on the related National, Provincial or County websites categorized by resource type & value. All bids & proposals shall also list the details of the parties making the proposal or bid & those approving the bid. Minor Resources shall be published on the County website, Medium Resources on the Provincial website & Major Level Resources shall be published on the National websites. Leases of Public-Resources may only be awarded to persons or Associations who will be utilizing the resource & not to brokers or resellers.

Article. Section.:12.5 Replacement Lease Proposal

When a solid Proposal is made by another party on an existing Lease that increases the overall returns of the people by at least twenty percent (20%) without any significant adverse effects to the community, economy or environment, the new proposal shall be approved by the Regions Board of Directors or people & replace the existing Lease. However, if the existing Lease Holder makes a counter proposal matching the new Replacement Lease Proposal, the existing Lease Holder will retain the Lease under the new terms. The twenty percent (20%) improvement should weigh up all factors of the lease including & quantifying factors such as maintaining or increasing jobs, improved environmental protection, lower-cost access to raw materials for the people etc. The former Lease Holder must be given a reasonable length of time to vacate the property, generally ninety (90) days. Replacement Lease Proposals must fairly meet any Restitution Clause requirements for any private assets remaining on the land that are transferred with the Lease. The term "solid Proposal" herein means a proposal that comes from a party who is capable of meeting the terms of their Proposal.

Article. Section.:12.6 Lease Proposal Approval

In approving a Lease Proposal, the total benefit of a Lease should be considered, including for example, job creation, low-cost raw materials, environment restoration, etc. Preference in awarding Leases should be given to those who are already effectively utilizing the property, & to those who can assure competence, such as qualified individuals, established businesses & productive farmers, while optimizing the citizens returns & ensuring the protection of the national heritage, economy & environment.

The voting for approval or disapproval of a Lease Proposal shall be publicly listed showing which Directors & Citizens cast or removed their vote. If more Citizens vote against a Lease Proposal than for it, the Lease Proposal shall be denied. Where more than a quarter of the Citizens in a region vote against a Lease Proposal, approval for the Lease must come from a majority of the People & not the Board of Directors.

A consecutive two-month majority vote of a County Board of Directors or a quarter or more of the Citizens in that County may approve a Lease for any Minor Public-Resource in their County, except where more Citizens vote to oppose verses approve the Lease.

A consecutive three-month majority vote of a Provincial Board of Directors or a quarter or more of the Citizens in that Province may approve a Lease for any Medium Public-Resource in their Province, except where more Citizens vote to oppose verses approve the Lease.

A consecutive four-month majority vote of a National Board of Directors or a quarter or more of the Citizens in the Nation may approve a Lease for any Major Public-Resource in their Nation, except where more Citizens vote to oppose verses approve the Lease.

After considering how solid a Proposal is, where equivalent Proposals are made for a Resource, preference shall firstly go to Citizens with Homesteads in the County & Associations with a majority of Citizen owners with Homesteads in the County, followed by Citizens & Associations from the Province, followed by Citizens & Associations from the Nation, followed by Citizens & Associations from other Universal Peopleisim Constitution Nations. Preference for Agricultural Resource Leases shall go to Citizens with agricultural experience & Homesteads on or adjacent to the agricultural Resource & any existing agricultural utilization.

Article. Section.:12.7 **Extractable Resources**

All Extractable Natural Resources such as minerals, water, forests, wireless spectrum, shall belong to the People. Any Citizen or Association who wishes to extract Natural Resources must make an Extraction Lease Proposal to the respective Board of Directors & People of the region. If they wish to take over an existing Lease they must make a Replacement Extraction Release Proposal.

The Lease terms for extracting natural resources shall be negotiated & approved by the Board of Directors or People of the region under the guidance of the Public-Resource Teams. Lease terms for extracted Resources must specify suitable environmental protections & that all extracted resources may only be sold on the Citizens-Services Trading & Banking System. Public-Resource Teams from a region must be given reasonable access to audit the extraction of Resource/s. Both the Resource Team & the party extracting the Resource/s shall independently report on the relative regions Board website at the end of each month the amount of the Resource/s extracted. The Lease Terms may either specify a percentage of profits from the sale of the extracted Resource, or a percentage of the sales price of the extracted Resource, be paid into the People's General-Fund. Leases which optimize the return to the people, must be favored.

Any person or Association who Leases land or has a Homestead on land with a significant extractable Natural Resource/s, may not unreasonably restrict the establishment & implementation of a Replacement Extraction Lease Agreement to extract the natural resource/s. Where the extraction of resources interferes with an existing land Lease or Homestead, the Citizen or Association owning the Homesteaded or leasing the land, must be fairly compensated for any remaining Free-Hold Lease and/or Homestead value, & for any immoveable assets they own on the land based on a fair Public-Resource Team assessment & implemented through a Replacement Lease Proposal in conformance with the "Regions & Boundaries of Universal Earth, Citizens Homestead" clause or Replacement Lease clause.

Citizens & Association who lawfully & fairly owned a mine during the transition to this Constitution must be given every opportunity to maintain a Free-Hold Lease on the land & establish a fair Extraction Lease Agreement to continue mining the Resource. Any Citizen or Association who makes a Replacement Extraction

Lease Proposal on a property with a Free-Hold Lease on the land, needs to pay the Free-Hold Lease holder a fair market value for the value of the remaining Free-Hold Lease on the land value alone, excluding any mineral or extractable resource value. Public-Resource Teams shall fairly determine the residual value of any Free-Hold Lease on the land, in addition to determining the Replacement Extraction Lease Agreement terms which must be approved pursuant to the terms of this Article.

Article. Section.:12.8   Assets & Resource Registry & Audits

All Minor Public-Resources in a County shall be registered, classified & published on the County websites along with all Approved Leases & Lease Proposals on the Resources. The County websites shall also list & link to the Medium & Major Public-Resources in the County listed on the Provincial & National websites.

All Medium Public-Resources in a Province shall be registered, classified & published on the Provincial websites along with all Approved Leases & Lease Proposals on the Resource. The Provincial websites shall also list & link to the Major Public-Resources in the Province listed on the National website.

All Major Public-Resources in a Nation shall be be registered, classified & published on the National websites along with all Approved Leases & Lease Proposals on the Resource.

All privately owned assets on Public Property shall be registered on the County websites. Registration shall take the form of a classification, description, photograph/s, date established & cost including clearly defined ownership of the asset. These assets must also be linked to the Public-Resource & or Lease Agreement which they are associated with.

Public-Resource Teams established by the County, Provincial & National Boards of Directors or the people, shall carry out ongoing audits of the Resources & Assets in their regions. The audits shall be conducted at suitable intervals or when a New or Replacement Lease Proposal needs to be considered. Details of the audits shall be published on the website where the Resource is listed. For Audits evaluating the value of Public-Resources & for evaluating the value of private registered immoveable assets affected by a Replacement Lease Proposal, Public-Resource Teams shall not be denied reasonable access to the Public-Resource & associated Asset/s.

Article. Section.:12.9   Failure to Make Lease Payments

Lease payments should be due on or before the first day of a lease period. Where a person or Association fails to make a lease payment, they must be noticed via email by a Board of Directors, or a Resource Team or the Citizen-Services System. If the Lease Holder fails to make the payment within thirty (30) days, another email notice in addition to a written notice, must be mailed via certified mail to the Lease Holder or placed on the primary entrance of the property or in the mailbox of the property. If the Lease Holder fails to make the payment within sixty (60) days, in addition to another email notice another written notice must be mailed via certified mail to the Lease Holder or placed on the primary entrance of the property or in the mailbox of the property. If the Lease

Holder fails to make a payment within ninety (90) days they may be evicted from the property. Following an eviction, any lease payments they failed to make while occupying the property, shall still be due. Where a Citizen or Association is experiencing an unusual hardship, they may appeal to a majority of the relative Board of Directors for additional time to make payments, or they may renegotiate the lease terms. The Board of Directors where the Public-Resource is registered shall be responsible for enforcing evictions & delivering the email & written notices with the assistance of the local County Board of Directors.

Article. Section.:12.10   Restitution

Wars & corrupt government, along with fraudulent fiat-money fractional-reserve banking, has resulted in extreme & unfair ownership of the land & businesses. This Constitution seeks to fairly turn all property, except Homesteads, over to the people for equal & equitable benefit, giving fair restitution where it is due. The transition to this New Constitution should not needlessly disrupt existing businesses & farms that are contributing to society.

The fraudulent fiat-money fractional-reserve banking systems having robed the people of their assets over the last century, must be reset & the people paid back restitution from the banks. Any & all banking debt on homes, vehicles, buildings & businesses shall be forgiven & recorded against the individual persons who benefited as restitution paid. As recovered assets stolen by the bankers are recovered, these assets shall be equally distributed to each Citizen, less that which they were forgiven in banking debt.

Public-Resource Teams shall calculate any restitution value for resources turned over to Public-Property or transferred with a Replacement Lease or forgiven in banking debt, all of which information shall be made public on the relative County, Provincial & National websites.

Property owners shall not be refused the right to establish their Homestead on property they lawfully & fairly owned during the transition to this Constitution. Where on the transition to this Constitution a Citizen or Association lawfully & fairly owned a property larger than their Homestead maximum, they shall be granted a one hundred (100) year Free-Hold Lease on the land, excluding any Bank loan on the property. Where a bank loan is held against a property, the percentage of the value of the loan verses the value of the property shall be deducted from the one hundred year Free-Hold Lease. The value of any Homesteaded portion of the property shall be excluded. Excluding the value of the Homesteaded portion of the property, if sixty percent (60%) of the non-Homesteaded property value is in the form of a bank loan, the Citizen owner shall receive a forty (40) year Free-Hold Lease on the remainder of the property. Any outstanding debt on the Homesteaded portion of the property shall conform to the "Citizens Free Banking, Voting, Trading, University & Courts (Citizen-Services" Article & "Equitable Elimination of Debt" Clause. A Free-Hold Lease shall require no monthly lease payments or tax & the remaining Free-Hold Lease may be sold by the Lease Holder. When a Free-Hold Lease expires, an approved Lease Proposal with lease payments shall be required.

Where a Citizen or Association has invested a significant amount in immovable assets on public land, their Lease costs must not be prohibitive, & the award of a Replacement Lease Proposal, needs to reasonably & fairly compensate them for the immovable asset value of the transferred assets. The owner of the assets may also lease their assets as part of the lease agreement to the new Lease Holder.

Properties belonging to religious institutions or institutions who benefited from tax free contributions, that have effectively been funded by the general populous, shall be turned over to the people & utilized for the community & those who contributed to their construction. The People & County Boards of Directors shall ultimately be responsible for fair allocation & use of these public facilities, which may, based on the County Board of Directors or People's decision, continue to be utilized free of any lease costs.

To receive restitution, owners must provide proof to the Public-Resource Teams as to how they obtained the property & the funds they used to purchase the property, all of which shall be made public on the relative County, Province and/or Nation's websites by the Public-Resource Team. Restitution must be just & equitable, reflecting an equitable balance between the public interest & the interests of those affected, having regard to all relevant circumstances, including: the current use of the property; the history of the acquisition & use of the property; the market value of the property; the relative value of fiat-money used to purchase the property; the value of the improvements on the property; discounted against any loans made with fractional-reserve fiat-money or inflated foreign currency.

There shall be no Restitution for property obtained through unfair transfer or acquisition, especially taking into account the use of fraudulent fiat-money, imbalanced foreign exchange, fractional-reserve banking, or property gained through wars & corrupt & unfair government transfers. All restitution for investments made with lawfully acquired foreign funds, will be calculated back to the exchange rate that existed before the currencies were detached from asset-backed gold or silver standards, also taking into considering political imbalances. The Restitution Advisory Board shall provide Public-Resource teams guidelines & software to calculate the value of fiat-money against grams of gold at the time.

Article. Section.:12.11   Restitution for Mines & Extracted Resources

The natural resources of the planet belong equally to all beings on the planet, both current & future generations. All natural resources save the Homesteads of the people, shall be turned over to the people. Where mines have been owned in the past by unfair grants issued by corrupt governments or purchased with money made by banking fraud or money stolen through wars or criminal racketeering, or in disregard to sharing the mineral wealth with the people, the mineral assets & or profits made from the sale of these assets that always belonged to the people, shall be recovered & restored to the people & all beings on this planet, both current & future generations, taking into account fair & generous pay & rewards to those who actually worked the mining operations.

Article. Section.:12.12   Public Utilities

Communities are responsible, as they always have been, for establishing & implementing Utilities. Utility guidelines & the promotion of advanced free-energy technologies shall be promoted at the National level by the Energy Advisory Board through a fund Citizens, Associations & Residents may voluntarily contribute to. With oversight from the Energy Advisory Board, public owned & the public portion of pseudo-public owned facilities & utilities, such as sewage, waste, electricity, communications entities, shall be turned over to the people & managed by the County Board of Directors & the Citizens of the County where they are based, who may decide to either establish Community owned Associations to manage & charge for services provided by the Facilities or provide these services free to the people, or to lease out Public Facilities to independent Associations to provide services to the community for a fee.

Article. Section.:12.13   Airports, Harbors, Roads & Rights-of-way

The Transport Board of Directors with whatever necessary cooperation from the National, Provincial & County Boards of Directors, may establish voluntary funds for the building & maintenance of existing & new airports, harbors, roads & rights-of-way across the Nation, or fund from reasonable use fees may be utilized for this purpose. Profitable Associations & wealthy Citizens who use the airports, harbors, roads or rights-of-way should contribute to these funds. Reasonable, non-obtrusively advertising may be used to raise money for these funds. Any person causing significant damage or significant ware to an airport, harbor, road, right-of-way or public property, may be liable to pay for that damage or use. Citizens & Residents may volunteer or be appointed by the Boards to manage & maintain airports, harbors, roads & rights-of-way as part of their Citizen & Resident Service. No roadblocks, tolls or any form that restricts travel may be setup at an airport, harbor or on a road or right-of-way, except that at points of entry to the Nation people & goods may be reasonably checked for conformance with the Border Management Article of this Constitution.

Article. Section.:12.14   Careful Consideration Of Pollution

In the approval of a Lease on a Public-Resource, or the removal of the approval, careful consideration in regard to the cost of cleanup from pollution must be taken into account by the Resource Teams, Boards of Directors & People. In all cases where any person or Association causing pollution, the cleanup costs must be born by the polluter. Pollution of the earth shall be strictly prohibited. Recycling of materials must in all instances, be promoted & where possible, enforced by the people & Boards of Directors.

Article. Section.:12.15   Peoples-Parks

The majority of Citizens or Board of Directors in a region may with a majority vote declare an area of pristine beauty, or high common recreational use, a Peoples-Park. The designation shall bare the title County, Provincial or National Peoples-Park. With the oversight of the Peoples-Parks Advisory Board, the Board of Directors & people from the County, Province or Nation that establishes the Peoples-Park, shall be responsible for governing & maintaining the park. Land declared as a Peoples-Park should wherever possible, be open & freely accessible to Citizens at all times, respecting the conservation & protection of the Park. Where there is an excessive demand for the use of a Peoples-Park, or where use threatens the natural beauty & ecology of the Peoples-Park, access may be governed according to terms setup & approved by a majority of the Peoples-Parks Advisory Board & the Board of Directors or people responsible for the park, giving preference to local Citizens. As for any Public-Resource, reasonable lease terms for use, may be established in the form of a usage fee. Access to Peoples-Parks may not be exclusive & may not exclude the general populous. Where a reservation system is required, Citizen-Services may provide standard on-line reservation systems for managing access to Peoples-Parks overseen by the Peoples-Parks Advisory Board.

Citizens enjoying a Peoples-Park have a duty to preserve the park & leave it in the same or better condition it was in when they arrived. It is a criminal act to cause any significant damage to a Peoples-Park. Citizens who observe anyone carrying out activities that are significantly damaging the Peoples-Park should record the criminal acts & may, to prevent further damage & or escape from liability, detain the criminal pursuant to the Due-Process Terms of this Constitution. Other than those with the express function of taking care of & managing the Park, no person should stay more than thirty (30) consecutive days in a Peoples-Park, & no more than one hundred & twenty (120) days per year.

Where significant valuable Extractable Resources are located in a pristine Peoples-Park, the return on public revenue from extracting the resources must be carefully weighed against ongoing enjoyment of future generations. Any Extraction Lease Agreement must ensure maximum ecological protection & the restoration of the Peoples-Park to its original pristine state.

Article. Section.:12.16 Public Health & Hospitals

Government run health-care institutions have a track record of inefficiency & abusive health-care. Competent medical professionals and/or medical Associations should be encouraged to lease at reasonable rates any existing public hospital infrastructure for establishing medical practices. With the oversight of the Medical Advisory Board, Boards of Directors, with the voluntary agreement & funding from people in their region, may also establish a community based & funded Medical Associations to assume the role of managing & funding existing or new community hospitals.

With oversight from the Medical Advisory Board, County or Provincial Boards of Directors may appoint Medical Administrative Committees to manage the allocation & scheduling of any free treatment of needy people in their region, all of which shall be public. The cost of medication & materials in the provision of any free medical treatment given by a medical professional as part of Citizen-Service, shall be reasonable & borne by the patient, & shall also be public, unless the County Board of Directors provides alternate voluntary funding. To establish incentive for health verses medical treatment, County Boards of Directors may set up medical insurance funds for people in their region to subscribe to, where selected medical professionals are paid to keep the people healthy, & where treatment of subscribers for any ailments that are not accidents or self-induced, is covered at the medical professionals expense.

Article. Section.:12.17   Educational Facilities

Government run educational institutions have a track record of poor quality & restrictive education. The typical State School's hypnotic & parrot like repetition in education, eliminates innovation, intelligent thought & creates slave-like drones, who can become a limitation or threat to civilized society.

Pursuant to the direction of the various Advisory Boards, Citizen-Services shall provide free digital education content & facilities for the people to educate themselves. Pursuant to the "Peopleisim General-Fund & Revenue Share" Article, Citizens aged eighteen (18) & under receive Revenue-Share each month for education & care, allowing the parents & children, their own choice in education.

In cooperation with the Educational Advisory Board, County Boards of Directors should appoint local Education Advisory Committee/s to manage the allocation & scheduling of educational professionals Community-Service & to allow children & adults to receiving excellent education in their County.

Educational professionals or Associations should be encouraged to lease at no cost or reasonable rates public owned educational infrastructure for establishing effective free or low cost education in the regions. The people & or County Boards of Directors, with voluntary agreement & funding from their community, may also establish community based & funded Associations to assume the role of managing existing or new community educational facilities. With the oversight of the Educational Board of Directors, educators & educational Associations approved by a majority of either the County, Provincial, National or International Board of Directors or people in their regions, who provide education, shall not be required pay any lease on the land they utilize for the sole purpose of education.

Article. Section.:12.18   Spectrum & Communications

The airwaves/spectrum belongs to the people. When this Constitution is established as the law of a region, the rights to all wireless spectrum shall revert back to the people in that region. The open use of spectrum shall be promoted & always take preference over private network use of spectrum. Digital technology has made the implementation of free public wireless networks feasible. Interconnecting public wireless networks shall be a National, Provincial & County priority focused on free Internet access. Subordinate to any vote of the people, the Communications Advisory Board along with the County, Provincial, National & International Boards shall manage & allocate wireless spectrum as a Public-Resource in the interest of the people & open communication. The Boards may assist in setting up & assist in managing open access wireless & wired networks across the Nation. The Board shall also interface & cooperate with the International Telecommunications Unions for international terrestrial, oceanic & satellite communications.

The Communications Advisory Board shall provide public guidelines on the use of wireless spectrum & interconnecting wireless public networks to terrestrial networks & work to phase out any private wireless networks in favor of open spectrum utilization. An open study relating the any harmful effects of wireless communications on people & the environment, shall also be established by the Communications Advisory Board for the purpose of guiding the effective non-obtrusive use of technology.

Any private Lease of wireless spectrum shall be subject to the Lease & Replacement Leases clauses of this Constitution. Any Association or person opening their private network to public traffic shall be entitled to reasonable compensation, determined & governed by the Communications Advisory Board of Directors to be paid from a voluntary fund for that purpose.

Using private or public networks to hack computers, spread viruses, snoop private information or any adverse activity that threatens open, free & non-obtrusive private communication by the people shall be a serious criminal offense; any person committing any of these offenses may be prosecuted by any affected Citizen or the Communications Board of Directors for criminal offenses & be held liable for three times the damage they caused, except where it can be proven without any reasonable doubt that such actions were genuinely carried out in the interests of the people to protect universal peace.

ARTICLE 13. CITIZENS FREE BANKING, VOTING, TRADING, UNIVERSITY & COURTS (CITIZEN-SERVICES)

A Citizens Free Banking, Voting, Trading, University & Court System, collectively called "Citizen-Services", shall be established as peoples not-for-profit Associations to deliver the various Citizen-Services in the various regions. Citizen-Services shall provide a universal asset-backed digital currency & banking system with a Peopleisim General-Fund into which & from which the peoples Revenue-Share is paid; trading systems & services; lease proposal registration, approval & collection systems; homestead & asset registration systems; voting systems; websites for the Counties, Provinces & Nation & the Boards; digital court systems; digital libraries; digital education systems. Under the oversight of the Citizen-Services Advisory Board & the Universal, International & National Boards, Citizen-Services shall be responsible for fairly & equitably distributing Citizens Revenue-Share benefits from the lease of Public-Resources & the sale of natural resources in addition to distribution of any restitution or recovered assets. All Peopleisim General-Fund transactions shall be publicly viewable. Citizen-Services shall not charge Citizens or Associations owned by Citizens any fees or interest for use of the system & the currency, & shall provide the following services & infrastructure:

- Website services for the various regions & Boards of Directors.
- Bank Accounts for each Citizen, Associations & Residents.
- Citizen Identity Registration & an Email address for each Citizen.

- Distribution of benefits to citizens from the lease of Public-Resources.
- Applications & secure Data Servers for:
    - Banking
    - Trading Systems
    - Ballots & Voting
    - Digital Common Law Courts
    - Digital Libraries & Education
    - Registering Homesteads
    - Registering Asset Ownership
    - Registering Public Resources
    - Registering Lease Proposals, Voting & Approvals on Leases
    - Recording Associations
    - Recording Copyrights
- Low cost or free computers for citizens to partake in & interact with Citizen-Services.

Article. Section.:13.1   Peopleisim General-Fund & Revenue-Share

Citizen-Services shall establish a Peopleisim General-Fund into which revenue for the people shall be paid, including revenue from Leases on Public-Resources, extracted Natural Resources, Penalties & all income generated in the name of the people. Under the oversight & direction of the National, International & Universal Boards of Directors, each month Citizen-Services shall distribute revenue paid into said Peopleisim General-Fund equitably to each eligible Homesteaded Citizen & their children. Only Citizens actively serving in a recognized Universal Peopleisim County, Province or Nation, & those lawfully exempt from service by a Board of Directors, shall be eligible to receive a share of the Peopleisim General-Fund distribution.

The Peopleisim General-Fund share for eligible Citizens children under the age of eighteen (18) shall be utilized for the care & education of the child. In the child's first nine (9) years the parents of the child shall be responsible for allocating their child's funds to pay for and/or save up for the education & care of the child. In the child's tenth (10th) year the child may decide how to distribute five (5%) percent of their annual funds to their own care & education while their parents manage the balance & any accumulated savings, in their eleventh (11th) year ten percent (10%), their twelfth (12th) year fifteen percent (15%), the thirteenth (13th) year twenty percent (20%), the fourteenth (14th) year twenty five percent (25%), the fifteenth (15th) year thirty percent (30%), the sixteenth year (16th) forty percent (40%), the seventeenth year (17th) fifty percent (50%), the eighteenth year (18th) sixty percent (60%). In their eighteenth (18th) year they may also sign this Constitution & receive their full distribution as an adult & manage any savings accumulated in their name. All distributions of funds to children shall be used only for education & direct care of the child & shall be viewable & monitored by the local County Board of Directors, parents & assigned guardians of the child. Where the County Board of Directors irrefutably determines that a parent is blatantly misappropriating a child's revenue share funds, by a majority vote of the Directors on the Board, pursuant to the due-process in this Constitution, the issue shall be brought through an administrative hearing, mediation & trial by jury if necessary, to determine a resolution or appointment of a responsible guardian by the Jury, who shall be liable for their actions. With Citizen-Services approval, at the County level, a majority of the people or a majority of the County Board of Directors may vote unanimously for three consecutive months to change the age / percentage of distribution of funds to Citizens children.

The County Board of Directors shall also be responsible for ensuring that Citizens in their region are not taken advantage of by the unscrupulous, & shall appoint counselors to advise & educate the needy in their region; & where the evidence is irrefutable & the crime obvious, prosecute any unscrupulous persons for any racketeering or crimes in their County.

Article. Section.:13.2   Establishing & Maintaining Citizen-Services

Following the establishment of Citizen-Services Banking in a region, fiat-money & fractional-reserve banking shall be illegal. Any person or organization that implemented or implements or supports fiat-currency & or fractional-reserve banking in any Peopleisim region, shall be prosecuted for fraud & their assets seized & handed over to Citizen-Services by a Jury following the due-process under this Constitution; All these seized funds, accounts & assets handed over to Citizen-Services shall be public & utilized for funding the implementation & deployment of Citizen-Services. Assets in excess of Citizen-Services needs assumed from banking fraud, shall be contributed to the people for education & in excess of that, in restitution pursuant to the Restitution clause of this Constitution. Where insufficient funds are available for providing acceptable Citizen-Services to a community, Citizen-Services may increase reserves of the Bank by no more than ten percent (10%) of the total annual Peopleisim General-Fund revenue in the first ten (10) years of operation in a region & no less than three percent (3%) the revenue of a region after that.

The proper use of the Citizen-Services shall be the responsibility of the Universal, International, National, Provincial & County Boards of Directors, Citizens & Residents. Citizen-Services services shall be provided in international English & where practical, other suitable languages. The initial team responsible for the design & implementation of Citizen-Services shall be Directed by the Founder & Architect of The Earth Plan & Universal Peopleisim Constitution. Once operational, with the oversight of the Citizen-Services Advisory Board, management of the system shall be the joint responsibility of the International & National Board of Directors & the people, all of which shall be open & public. Citizen-Services shall be established to be self regulating with multiple levels of redundancy for security & reliability with transaction transparency to ensure integrity along with & public auditing of the system & transactions. All transactions on Citizen-Services shall be publicly viewable pursuant to the terms of this Constitution. Citizen-Services shall ensure that neither the currency nor any assets of the bank or those traded on Citizen-Services, are utilized in any way for making war.

Article. Section.:13.3   Equitable Elimination of Debt

Conforming to the "Leasing Peoples Resources & Recognition of Private Assets" Article & "Restitution" Clause of this Constitution, where a person owes money to a bank that is assumed by the Citizen-Services Bank, their debt shall be forgiven & recorded as paid out restitution, to be deducted from any future restitution payments. Where the Citizen-Services Bank & a Board of Directors clearly determines that the amount of debt forgiven any individual or Association on transition to this Constitution, is far in excess of any expected future restitution payments, pursuant to the Restitution Clause & due-process under this Constitution, with the relevant Board of Director & Public-Resource Team guidance, the asset shall be turned over to the public as a Public-Resource, to be sold or leased with proceeds going to the Peopleisim General-Fund. With any future debt of an individual or Association, where the Citizen-Services Bank & a Board of Directors clearly determine that the amount of debt owed, is well beyond what the debtor is reasonably capable of paying, following the due-process under this Constitution, the asset shall be turned over to the public as a Public-Resource to be sold or leased with proceeds going to the Peopleisim General-Fund. In extenuating circumstances, with a majority vote from the relevant Board of Directors or people, the Citizen-Services Bank shall have the authority to forgive debt. The Citizen-Services Bank shall treat all people with dignity & respect. No interest may ever be charged on financial debt.

ARTICLE 14.   BORDER MANAGEMENT

Article. Section.:14.1   Visitors: Tourists, Students & Business

All visitors, including tourists, business visitors & students, shall be welcome so long as they respect & do not violate any of the laws of this Constitution. To gain entry & travel through the Nation visitors must be invited & sponsored by a respectable local Citizen who knows them sufficiently to personally accept responsibility & liability for ensuring the visitor does not abuse the Nations goodwill, obeys the law & moves on back to their country of origin after a reasonable visit. Other than registered students on the campus of legitimate educational institutions, visitors shall not stay in one location for more than three (3) months or the country for more than a year without a majority of the local County Board of Directors permission & approval to be a Resident in the area they wish to stay longer im. A Citizen who sponsors a visitor that does not obey the law or respect the Constitution, with the assistance of the Tourism Board, Security Advisory & any local Boards, shall be responsible for evicting the visitor from the Nation. If negligent the sponsor of a visitor may be held liable for damage the visitor causes. If a visitor causes a significant problem the Citizen who sponsored them shall not be entitled to sponsor any further visitors. Visitors shall report at least once a week to their Citizen sponsor & Tourism Advisory Board in regard to their whereabouts & activities. When a Citizen looses contact with the visitor they sponsor for more than two weeks, the Citizen shall immediately notify the Tourism Advisory Board where they suspect the visitor may be, & fully cooperate with any Boards requests relating to the visitor. If they believe the visitor may have become a security risk they must advise & receive both the Tourism & the Security Advisory Boards acknowledgment of this advice.

Article. Section.:14.2 Residents

A Resident is a non Citizen who lives permanently or semi-permanently in a County where they lease property approved by a majority vote of a County Board of Directors or a majority of the people in the County. Any Resident who leases property must be formally registered as a Resident at the County level with the County Boards of Director oversight. Full details of all Residents & leases shall be publicly viewable on the appropriate Boards of Directors websites.

Article. Section.:14.3 Refugees Seeking Asylum

Political refugees who seek asylum must obtain permission from a majority vote by a County Board of Directors to temporarily move onto land designated & limited in purpose by the County Board of Directors for their specific use. Applications may be made directly to any County Board of Directors & shall be publicly listed on the County website.

Article. Section.:14.4 Customs & Importing Goods

There will be no duty on imported or exported goods other than the duty to ensure that what comes into the land is beneficial & not detrimental to the land & people. Imported goods must not possess any inherent threat or danger to people & the environment. Goods prohibited from import include:

- Any weapons of mass destruction, including atomic & biological weapons.
- Poisons that are not ecologically sound.
- Genetically Modified products & seeds that are known or suspected to cause health risk.
- Non germinating seeds.
- Non Citizens may not import or carry any weapons.

The Security Advisory Board & County Boards of Directors at ports & points of entry to their County shall assign inspection duty to Citizens in their County who shall where necessary politely, efficiently & expediently inspect any imported goods & visitors for compliance with this Article & Constitution. Any & all Citizens have authority to inspect situations where they have good & reasonable grounds & suspicion to believe a person is in violation of these importation restrictions, however, not without observing all Constitutional due-process. Typical inspections should not take longer than five minutes & should not be obtrusive, unless the importer or visitor causes delay. Any case where a Citizen finds solid evidence that imported goods pose a serious risk, shall immediately be brought to the attention of the Security Advisory Board & three or more of the local County Board of Directors, who within forty eight hours (48h) shall have an Administrative Meeting with the importer to determine if the goods may or may not be imported or if further inspection & determination is required. Pursuant to the Due Process of this Constitution a Mediation session shall start as soon as possible with the importer & the County Board of Directors & Citizen Inspectors to attempt to resolve the issues if it cannot be resolved in the Administrative Meeting. If the mediation does not resolve the importation issues, the importer my request a trial by jury to authorize or deny the importation. The jury may order the goods be destroyed or returned to their origin. Details of the importer & goods denied importation shall be published on a website setup by the Security Advisory Board for this purpose. Importers who have ever been denied the right to import goods must declare said denial for any goods they import into any other County or Peopleisim region.

ARTICLE 15. POLICE & MILITARY POWER

A well educated & armed populous is generally a safe populous. The strict enforcement of ranks in any organization creates artificial authority, oppression, barriers to liberty, lack of free thought, limited innovation & insane behavior. Studies & practice repeatedly reveal that when people are put in authority, they abuse that authority, especially in prisons & with the police & military. Many soldier or policeman's conscience is sheared with the insane ancient mythical preaching that sacrifice can wash away sin or grant power. The establishment of standing armies & armed police invariably leads to violent outcomes.

The people shall make up the police & military power of the Nation. There shall be no permanent military force nor any permanent police force. No atomic or biological weapons shall be developed, maintained or held by any person or entity in any of the Peopleisim regions.

Private security Associations may provide local security services for the people, however, no such private security Association may form an army or posses large caliber weapons or weapons designed for mass killing or destruction of buildings, such as explosives, tanks or fighter aircraft. When more than half a County or one quarter of a Province vote to disarm any individual or group in their region, the group or individual shall immediately get rid of all their weapons or leave the region.

Article. Section.:15.1 Identifying The Enemy

One of the greatest dangers & threats is not being able to identify the real enemy. To conquer a Nation, usually it must first be divided from within, against itself. Enemies inside a Nation are the most dangerous. Conflict is generally initiated by individuals or a small minority. The media, religion, racial intolerance, economic oppression, corrupt courts, State schools, secret societies such as the Jesuits & Masons, & the empowerment of evil individuals in government, along with false-flag operations, are most often employed to divide a people & make war. Rome/The Vatican & the old Roman Inner City-State of London/The Crown, have been responsible for instigating most wars over the last millennium. Loosely referred to as the Illuminati, these same powers, including the Nazi 3rd Reich &

New Rome's 4th Reich a.k.a. New Rome/Washington D.C, funded by the owners of the US Federal Reserve Bank, Bank of England & the Vatican's Bankers, have been responsible for instigating most wars over the last millennium. The Jesuits, Masons, Nazi SS, KGB & the CIA, have been the primary secret gangs used to instigate wars by dividing Nations from within & in assassinating anyone who opposes their evil plans. However, the most effective means of invasion has not been with weapons, it has been with money literally made out of nothing called "fiat-money". The owners of the private US Federal Reserve Bank, World Bank, BIS, along with other privately owned Central Banks & their franchise banks, have used their fiat-money & fractional-reserve banking to take control of governments, political parties, the media, military, police, judiciary, corporations, peoples homes & assets. Where the Illuminati can not take control of a nations money supply & government, they cause internal conflict utilizing Jesuits, Masons & the CIA & finally invade with the US/New Rome's Army. TV & radio programming along with God & religion have been Rome's primary principles used to hypnotize & paralyze individuals into controllable states of stupor. The Security Advisory Board shall be responsible of ensuring all the people are well educated in regard to these issues.

Article. Section.:15.2 Effective Counter Measures

It is extremely difficult to stir up discontent in a content educated populous.

Eliminating poverty with Peopleisim Revenue-Share, & giving people security on the land with their Homestead, & stabilizing the economy by eliminating the private ownership of banks & the private banks ability to make money out of nothing with Citizen-Services Bank, people controlled education & open access to knowledge (elimination of Gag-Orders on Patents), & providing the people with effective means to educate themselves, provide effective counter measures to violence & war, bringing contentment & civilization.

The use of modern weapons such as missiles, drones & biological weapons, makes armies & traditional weapons ineffective against conventional armed forces attacks. One of the most powerful weapons today, is the camera & ability to expose to the world any atrocity or aggression, especially when the horrors are exposed to the people within the offending Nation. Effective new media through Internet can ward off an invasion. Ensuring that Internet is open without censorship is critical.

Citizens in the US never see the actual impact on lives the bombs they pay for cause. Few know the US Federal Reserve Bank is a private bank, even less know that it is owned by an international criminal banking cartel responsible for instigating most of the wars, recessions & depressions for personal profit. Hardly any know Washington D.C. was founded on a Roman Catholic Jesuit colony literally called "New Rome". As a consequence of State-schools, many young people don't even know the Roman Catholic Jesuits were responsible for the Inquisition, they don't even know what the Inquisition was. Young people are starting to realize Washington D.C. carried out the 9/11 terrorist attacks & that the bankers are are criminals.

Waking up people from inside an aggressive Nation like the US is key. Exposing their governments violence, coupled with commercial pressure against an offending Nation & its people, can be more powerful than any military weapon. Should US Citizens who fund Washington D.C./New Rome with tax, be allowed to travel or do business internationally? Should the guilty bankers not be indicted, arrested & prosecuted for fraud?

Citizens must be encouraged to publish the truth & expose false-flag events along with who exactly is behind & benefiting from any conflict. Exposure of the CIA, Catholic, Jesuit & Masonic involvement in wars over the last centuries will help eliminate these criminal gangs. Few realize that Roman Catholics not only instigated the Crusades, but that they also educated Mohamed & instigated Islam, backed Napoleon, the British Crown, the Nazi's, Hitler & Washington D.C. The use of religion as a dividing force, has been one of the primary tools for conflict, initiated & funded by Romes' bankers such as the Rothschild family. Avoiding the Criminal Banking Cartels use of fiat-money, especially the US Dollar & also the Euro, prevents foreign bankers from buying a Nation & enslaving its people with fiat-money they literally make out of nothing. Recognizing that the World Bank is a financial terrorist & avoiding it's loans is critical.

Supporting, defending & backing whistle-blowers who publish & expose corruption, should be activities every Citizen personally & actively engages in. Eliminating government, large corporate & foreign ownership of media is crucial. Encouraging individual authorship & media production, along with open Internet, is key.

It is necessary to identify & indict known individuals & secret-societies involved in terrorist activities such as the Vatican, Washington D.C., the English Crown, the Rothschild's, the Jesuit & Masonic secret-societies & others, & to indict, arrest & prosecute these criminals for their crimes. When these international terrorists enter any region they should be immediately arrested & prosecuted. All assets belonging to these Illuminati criminals who have been instrumental in instigating the wars, genocide & recessions, need to be confiscated & returned to the people.

Conflict & war is started by dividing from within. This Universal Peopleisim Constitution unites the people as one. As one we cannot be divided.

ARTICLE 16. POWER & ENERGY PRODUCTION & SUPPLY

With the assistance of the Energy Advisory Board, free & sustainable energy sources & solutions shall be identified & promoted by all Boards of Directors. No gag-orders on energy technology shall be allowed or enforced. Any actions or attempts to buy-out or suppress free-energy technology shall be strictly prohibited & charged with high treason. No power systems that produce dangerous waste or radioactive waste or serious risks of catastrophic explosions shall be permitted. All State & large private power generation shall be turned over to the people.

ARTICLE 17.   ORGANIZATIONS & GREED

Article. Section.:17.1   Recognized Entities

Corporations, trusts & other entities shall cease to exist & may be freely transferred to Citizen owned Peopleisim Associations conforming to this Constitution. Associations shall consist of a collective of identifiable individual persons or Peopleisim Associations who may own various types of shares in the Association & who's owners shall ultimately be responsible for the Associations actions. Associations shall respect the rights, maxims & due-process established by this Constitution. Associations management structure, stock structure & voting may follow any form so long as the owners of the Association are identifiable for the liability of the Association.

Article. Section.:17.2   Monopolies

Monopolies in business & services shall be prohibited. The most effective means to eliminate a monopoly is for the people to band together & refuse to support a monopoly. Where by the vote of a majority of the people in a region, a person or Association or foreign Corporation, is determined to be an unhealthy monopoly, the people may vote to limit the monopoly in their region as they choose. By a resolution approved by a majority of the National Board of Directors, any Association that controls more than seventy five percent of a large National market shall be split in two, with separate non-associated ownership in each half. When separate Associations can be shown to be colluding to fix market prices they may be considered as one & treated as a monopoly.

Article. Section.:17.3   Realization Of Amassed Fortune

A *Realization of Amassed Fortune,* is the assumption, by the people, of a greedy individuals grossly excessive assets to be distributed & shared equally amongst all Citizens in the same manner in which proceeds from Public-Resources are distributed. A person that amasses fortunes in excess of the equivalent value of ten tons of gold (10,000 kgG) to themselves, can be subject to a *Realization of Amassed Fortune* after one half of a Province's voters vote for a *Realization of Amassed Fortune* against the greedy persons assets in that Province. The Restitution Advisory Board shall govern any *Realization of Amassed Fortune* with oversight & assistance from other Boards.

Article. Section.:17.4   Birth Control

It is the duty of every Citizen to respect the fact that over population is a serious problem & that they have a birth control duty to the planet. Under the guidance of the Medical & Health Advisory Boards, the County Boards of Directors should ensure that low cost & safe sterilization & birth control solutions are available in their regions.

When the forth (4) child is born to a person, their right to a Homestead passes to their children & they must live on their child's Homestead or leased land. If none of their children have reached the age of eighteen they may utilize the future Homestead right of the forth child until that child is of age. If none of their adult children will allow them to live on their land & the parent is destitute, they shall have the right to a homestead of twenty five square meters. When the sixth (6) child is born to a person their right to any Revenue-Share or distribution form the Peopleisim General-Fund shall be eliminated & they will have to rely on their own income or the generosity of their adult children to take care of them.

ARTICLE 18.   UNIVERSAL MATTERS

Mankind is finally waking up to the fact that humans are merely one species in a universe teaming with life & many other significantly more advanced extraterrestrial species & civilizations. The Old World Order that now calls itself the New World Order intentionally censored these universal facts in order to keep mankind ignorant & believing in myths that subjected them to obey imaginary gods. In 2001 "The Disclosure Project", amongst many other disclosures by highly respectable & credible leaders, coupled with irrefutable evidence revealed the fact that the governments of the past have intentionally censored evidence of extraterrestrial life & civilizations. It is now well known that there are many extraterrestrial civilizations, some of which visit planet earth & some of whom have had dealings with governments & people on earth.

Article. Section.:18.1   Extraterrestrials

No person or entity shall be prohibited with dealing with extraterrestrials, however, any such dealing shall be publicly announced & fully disclosed to the Extraterrestrial Advisory Board & the local County, Provincial & National Board of Directors in the regions of interaction or observation, & on public & private websites designed for that purpose. The Extraterrestrial Advisory Board & Universal Board of Directors shall be responsible for monitoring & publicizing any & all important extraterrestrial activity on earth they are aware of. Any extraterrestrial seeking Citizenship shall be subject to extra scrutiny pursuant to the terms of nationalization in this Constitution & must be approved by a majority vote of each of the Boards of Directors in whose territory they wish to reside from the County Board of Directors to the Universal Board of Directors.

It is important to recognize that extraterrestrial civilizations have been visiting the earth for hundreds of thousands, if not millions of years, without any significant assault on mankind. As with all life, extraterrestrials are also to be respected & loved. Any person shooting at, harming or assaulting other beings who are not doing them any harm must be prosecuted for criminal assault.

Article. Section.:18.2   Human Health & Animal Rights

During the 1800's & 1900's & early 2000's, ninety percent of the planets non-human animals have literally been killed & eaten by humans, largely as a consequence of out-of-control greed, primitive religious beliefs & lies promoted by meat boards, coupled with a psychotic lack of consciousness amongst mankind. Most humans are not even aware that spinach has nearly twice to three times more protein than animal meat. Heart attacks, largely caused by eating meat, have became one of the leading causes of death in mankind. We pledge to correct this mindless horror & destruction. No being shall be subject to cruelty.

Advice from the worlds most intelligent people regarding eating meat reflects the reality:

> "Nothing will benefit human health & increase chances for survival of life on Earth as much as the evolution to a vegetarian diet." - Albert Einstein

> "On general principles the raising of cattle as a means of providing food is objectionable. It is certainly preferable to raise vegetables, & I think, therefore, that vegetarianism is a commendable departure from the established barbarian habit. That we can subsist on plant food & perform our work even to advantage is not a theory but a well-demonstrated fact." - Nikola Tesla,

> "[Vegetarianism has a] powerful influence upon the mind & its action, as well as upon the health & vigor of the body. Until we stop harming all other living beings, we are still savages." - Thomas Edison

> "There is no doubt that some plant food, such as oatmeal, is more economical than meat, & superior to it in regard to both mechanical & mental performance. Such food, moreover, taxes our digestive organs decidedly less, & in making us more contented & sociable, produces an amount of good difficult to estimate. In view of these facts every effort should be made to stop the wanton, cruel slaughter of animals, which must be destructive to our morals." - Nilola Tesla

> Other avid vegetarians include: Isaac Newton, Leonardo Da Vinci, Srinivasa Ramanujan, Edward Witten, Brian Greene & the Founder & Architect of Peopleisim.

ARTICLE 19. OFFICE LOCATIONS, FLAG & SEAL

Article. Section.:19.1 Location

There will be no State Capital nor any Provincial or County Capitals. Virtual office locations for the various Boards shall be published by the Boards, who will notify Citizens in their region as necessary. Physical offices may be located at any & multiple locations in the universe as determined by the various Boards of Directors, who's locations shall be listed on their websites. The official electronic mailing contact address' of any Board of Directors, shall be posted on each Board of Directors websites.

Article. Section.:19.2 Seal & Flag

By a majority vote, Counties, Provinces & Nations may choose whatever seal & flag they wish.

ARTICLE 20. TRANSITION

In order to effect a smooth effective transition from the old form of Stateism, Capitalism, Communism or Socialism to Peopleisim, the following measures are enacted:

Article. Section.:20.1 Transition Training Teams

To manage the smooth transition to a Peopleisim based government, transition teams shall be established to train & oversee the new Board of Directors & Citizens in the various regions. This transition training shall be funded by the people & any assets seized from banks & the former government.

Article. Section.:20.2 Treason

After a majority of the people in a region have signed their name to this Constitution, the County or Province or Nation shall come under the Universal Peopleisim Constitution law. The former police, prosecutors, magistrates, judges & government in that region must by law stand down. Any individual who attempts to continue in their roles for the former government, commits treason against this Constitution & is subject to indictment & prosecution for treason, which may be initiated by any Citizen in the region. In order to facilitate a smooth transition, individuals who held positions in the former government should be placed on formal Notice by any Citizen & preferably by a large group of Citizens, so they have the opportunity to comprehend the former government who employed them is no longer in charge & the ramifications of committing treason against the new law.

Where an former government official threatens violence or attempts to arrest or prosecute any Citizen under the former law, that official may be immediately detained by any Citizen who shall form a Grand Jury to Indict the accused within 24 hours. The Grand Jury shall determine the relative threat the accused poses to determine if they need to be held for the Administrative Hearing, Mediation & Trial by Jury pursuant to the due-process of this Constitution.

Where the threat is great, with the guidance of the Security Advisory Board, the County, Provincial & National Boards of Directors shall coordinate with all Universal Peopleisim Constitution regions to establish & carry out effective defense strategies. Where the threat is immediate, such as foreigners shooting at Citizens, it is perfectly reasonable to shoot back in defense, however, taking into careful consideration the Defense Strategy & methods promoted in this Constitution to establish peace & non-violence.

Article. Section.:20.3 Declaration Of Independence & War Against Those Who Make War Against Us & Order To Stand Down

We solemnly declare our independence & war against those who make war against us & their agents, employees & officers. We declare war against any State or nefarious organization & persons who engage in any of the following acts of war against us & order they stand down & cease & desist:

1. Inciting war for personal gain & profit & in carrying out false-flag operations for that purpose.
2. Invading other Nations & stealing the land & natural resources.
3. Taxing us & using our money to implement a corrupt police-state & corrupt courts to oppress us.
4. Enforcing fraudulent fiat-money on us made out of nothing by private banks & allowing usury.
5. Allowing banks to steal our natural resources, homes & businesses with fiat-money & fractional-reserve banking.
6. Establishing codes that prosecute non-crime as crime.
   (For every crime all three elements of a crime must be present: the Act, Intent & Damage).
7. Hiring both the prosecutor & the judge who prosecute cases against us & also judge the case. (A judge who has a personal interest, a gain or a relationship to any party in a case, is in excess of jurisdiction & commits a very serious criminal act tantamount to treason).
8. Controlling education & the curriculum & media to dumb us down & make us subservient.
9. Promoting Roman religions based on ancient myths to mislead the masses & make war.
10. Killing to satisfy greedy corporate & personal gain.
11. Promoting & forcing on us mind numbing chemicals such as fluoride, lead-mercury in fillings, excessive aluminum in deodorants & food, harmful vaccinations, spraying us with chemtrails, genetically modifying food to harm us, & other intentional assaults.
12. Utilizing media to hypnotize us for nefarious purposes & to incite war & hatred.
13. Censoring extraterrestrial civilizations & life throughout the universe to keep us ignorant.
14. Censoring free-energy & anti-gravity technology for the interests of oil & power companies & in placing gag-orders on patents to prevent human advancement.
15. Causing our impoverishment & enslavement in involuntary servitude to foreign owned banks who control political parties & governments by recruiting traitors & the ignorant from amongst us.

We recognize that the best way to stop war, is through universal consciousness that simply does not accept war & does not allow international criminal cartels to own our central banks & make money out of nothing & to prevent governments from using taxes to build armies & militarized police. The strong will of the collective masses, is often all that is necessary to force criminals out of governance & stop war. Refusing to cooperate with corrupt government, shuts down a small minority's control of that government. Those who pay tax to a government that is engaged in terrorism & crimes, themselves engage in &

support terrorism & crime. Scorn alone against those working for these terrorist governments, can alone help stop traitors amongst us from being used against us. In order to enslave a people, slaves are need to be recruited from amongst the people as slave drivers.

Article. Section.:20.4   Smooth Transition Of Governance & Law

It is imperative to maintain an ordered & peaceful transition to this Universal Peopleisim Constitution. Violence must be carefully avoided. It is important to recognize that this peaceful reformation can be disrupted by agents who infiltrate the movement for the express purpose of causing violence so that for example, the outgoing State can institute a State of Emergency & Martial Law. Citizens should arrest & prosecute any person amongst them who instigates violence.

The criminal cartels who own the central banks have militarized the police for the express purpose of enforcing Martial Law. In many regions they have even prepared Concentration Camps to crush any movement that threatens their control of government & ability to make money out of nothing which they utilize to enslave us & steal our resources. If the people stand together in the formation of this new constitution, the people will not fail. As soon as a majority of the people sign this Constitution in a region the former government's police are forced to stand down by law & their lawful authority is eliminated.

Article. Section.:20.5   Recovery Of Stolen National Assets

The Nation has been plundered by foreign outlaws who have used money they literally make out of nothing to steal what belongs to the people. These stolen assets shall be recovered to the people & those responsible for the theft brought to justice.

Article. Section.:20.6   Recovery Committees

The Restitution Advisory Board in cooperation with the various Boards of Directors shall establish teams to recover stolen assets to the people. As with all public operations & information, said Committees shall make all their dealings, findings & information publicly accessible on Internet. Said Committees may establish reasonable funding of their recovery operations which shall not exceed half the value of the assets they recover & should preferably amount to two percent of the value of the assets they recover. The Boards of Directors shall attempt to recover the stolen assets at no cost to the people so that their full value may be equally be distributed to the people.

Article. Section.:20.7   Asset Recovery Bounty

A bounty of two percent of the value of an asset recovered shall be paid to any third party who recovers stolen assets to the people. If the cost of recovery of said assets exceeds two percent, a bounty shall be negotiated prior to payment with a majority vote from the Restitution Advisory Board of Directors. Said bounty shall in no cases exceed fifty percent of the value of the asset.

Article. Section.:20.8   Fiat-Monetary Banking Fraud

Banks have committed fraud in the production & use of fiat-money that is not backed by anything & they have even charged usury interest on this fiat-money. Any bank involved in such fraud shall have all their assets seized & utilized for the establishment & operations of Citizen-Services in service of the people.

Article. Section.:20.9   Temporary Money

Regions who do not have access to the Citizen-Services banking services may utilize existing fiat-money systems until the Citizen-Services banking is establish in their region, or they may use temporary IOU Notes to facilitate basic commerce in their region. These temporary IOU Notes should preferably not be for large amounts & are in effect an "I Owe You" Note; All IOU Notes should be produced in duplicate, identifying clearly the date, the person issuing the Note & to Whom it is issued, a description of the goods exchanged, with the signature of both parties on the Notes, one to be kept by the buyer & one for the seller. With the two duplicate copies of the IOU Notes, balance of payments will be credited to each party on the Citizen-Services banking system when it is available with oversight by the various Boards of Directors & Public Resource Teams. The valuation on the temporary IOU Notes should be denominated in grams of gold (gG).

Article. Section.:20.10   Payback For Launch Contributions

Significant Donors who register their donation in support of launching this Universal Peopleisim Constitution with an approved written receipt from the board@theearthplan.com, may claim back double the financial amount donated for assisting in launching Peopleisim once a Universal Peopleisim Constitution region is established & generating sufficient returns from asset recovery or Leases from Public-Resources to pay them back. Any broker who assists in raising a significant amount of capital for these registered donations will be paid five percent (5%) commission.

Article. Section.:20.11   Prison Industrial Complex & Justice

Criminal racketeering has been common practice amongst the former governments who prosecuted people for non crimes to benefit themselves, lawyers & the prison industrial complex with jobs & income. Where a person was prosecuted for a non-crime in which there was no damage to a real party of interest who filed or files a verified criminal complaint, their conviction shall be reversed, if they are incarcerated they shall be immediately released. Victims of criminal racketeering & malicious prosecution may prosecute those who prosecuted them & are entitled to restitution for damages. Any person who was prosecuted in a case where the judge & prosecution were both employed by the State, & without any undue pressure they did not in writing consent to the trial, they shall be entitled to Due Process pursuant to this Constitution in an expedient manner taking into account reasonable delays caused as a consequence of the transition to this Constitution. The County Board of Directors with the guidance of the Due Process, Badlands & Restitution Advisory Boards shall ensure any victims of injustice in their region are afforded expedient justice in this regard.

Article. Section.:20.12 Victims of Wars & Oppression

Members of the Roman Catholic Church, Vatican, Jesuits, Masons, Knights of Malta, Yale Bones Club, CIA, Counsel on Foreign Relations, military, police & other organizations & individuals having been directly involved in instigating & carrying out war may be prosecuted for said criminal acts & held liable for paying restitution to the victims by any victim/s or person/s who competently represent a victim or victims. All assets & land stolen in war shall be returned to the rightful owners & where no victim can be found, to the people equally. Any person or organization who fails to immediately return stolen assets in their possession or control to the victim/s, or people if the victim/s cannot be found, shall be implicated in & also held accountable for the act of war or crime. The concept of sovereign immunity or authority is void in this Constitution.

Live, Love, oppose Evil

www.ingramcontent.com/pod-product-compliance
Lightning Source LLC
Chambersburg PA
CBHW060438290526
45791CB00002B/983